Your Towns and Cities

Dorking
in the Great War

After an MPhil in 17th Century Studies, Kathy wrote much of 'H' as assistant editor at the Oxford English Dictionary. She then spent 10 years as a city lawyer.

She is currently responsible for exhibitions at Dorking Museum and regularly leads guided walks and speaks on local history in the Dorking area. She has published three books of local history and is currently researching a book on the lives of the suffragette campaigners Frederick and Emmeline Pethick-Lawrence and the fight for the vote in the Surrey Hills.

Kathy runs regular guided tours to Ypres and the Somme, and has been able to combine her interest in the First World War with the history of Dorking in the preparation of this book.

Your Towns and Cities in the Great War

Dorking
in the Great War

Kathryn Atherton

Pen & Sword
MILITARY

First published in Great Britain in 2014 by
PEN & SWORD MILITARY
an imprint of
Pen and Sword Books Ltd
47 Church Street
Barnsley
South Yorkshire S70 2AS

ISBN 978 1 47382 552 9

A CIP record for this book is available from the British Library

Printed and bound in England
by CPI Group (UK) Ltd, Croydon, CR0 4YY

Typeset in Times New Roman by Chic Graphics

Pen & Sword Books Ltd incorporates the imprints of
Pen & Sword Archaeology, Atlas, Aviation, Battleground, Discovery,
Family History, History, Maritime, Military, Naval, Politics, Railways,
Select, Social History, Transport, True Crime, Claymore Press,
Frontline Books, Leo Cooper, Praetorian Press, Remember When,
Seaforth Publishing and Wharncliffe.

For a complete list of Pen and Sword titles please contact
Pen and Sword Books Limited
47 Church Street, Barnsley, South Yorkshire, S70 2AS, England
E-mail: enquiries@pen-and-sword.co.uk
Website: www.pen-and-sword.co.uk

Contents

Acknowledgements and Thanks   7

1   An Edwardian Market Town   9
     The Battle of Dorking   29

2   1914: Recall and Recruitment   31
     Missing in Action: Henry Harman Young   62
     A Military Family at War: The Heaths of Anstie Grange   63

3   1915: Invasions   67
     Do You Remember Suvla Bay, Sir?   97
     M. Gilbert's War   98
     Mr Vanderbilt and the *Lusitania*   99
     Ralph Vaughan Williams: the Composer in Wartime   103
     John Stavridi and Greek Neutrality   104

4   1916: Conscription, Exemption and Objection   106
     The Holmbury St Mary Prisoner of War Camp   122
     Despair and Suicide   122
     Boy Soldiers: Valentine 'Joe' Strudwick and Aubrey
          Hudson   123
     The Anstie Grange Military Hospital   126

**5   1917: Rationing, the Red Cross and the 'East End
          Foreigner'**   129
     The Diary of Kenneth Harman Young   144

The Pethick-Lawrence: Pacifists in the 'War to end
     all Wars'   144

6 1918: Armistice   150
      Growing Belladonna   157
      Charles Robertson VC   157
      Miss Daisy Wadling's Military Funeral   160
      'Sammy' Soane and Edith Withall   161

7 Memorials and Remembrance   163
      The Cubitt Boys   182
      A Peace Celebration Romance   184

Bibliography   185

Index   187

Acknowledgements and Thanks

This book has grown out of my research for a project with Dorking Museum & Heritage Centre to assess the impact of the First World War on the town of Dorking and the surrounding villages, and to present an exhibition in each of the centenary years of the war on a different aspect of it. Without the volunteers of the museum having dug deep into the museum's archives, the wealth of material on which it is based would not have been unearthed. Thanks in particular must go to Susannah Horne, Rachel Devine, Rebecca Stevenson, Harriet Parker, Jane le Cluse and Bobbie Rounthwaite. Lydia and Andy Burnham contributed essential newspaper research. Simon Jervis, Lorraine Spindler and Timothy Richardson have provided information on the military and on serving individuals. Much of the material relating to the village of Newdigate is based on the invaluable research of John Callcut. Thanks are also due to Mary Day and Bernice Forsyth for sharing their research on the village of Capel; to J.J. Heath-Caldwell for providing information on the Heath family; to the Vaughan Williams Society for information on the composer; and to all of those who have allowed the reproduction of images, many of whom have also added information.

Most of the photographs and archival material reproduced in this book are from the collection of Dorking Museum & Heritage Centre; Clare Flanagan has provided essential assistance in sourcing images. Permission to use these images is gratefully acknowledged.

Personal thanks for moral and physical support are due to Erica Chambers, Yvonne Brown, Peter Camp and my family: Richard, Tom and Ulysses Fedrick, and Don and Betty Attwood. My apologies for everything.

Copyright notice

Charity fundraisers in fancy dress at Dorking Hospital Saturday, which was held on 25 July 1914, just a few days before the outbreak of war.

CHAPTER 1

An Edwardian Market Town

In 1914 Dorking was a market town of 8,000 inhabitants. It was the focal point for a scattered agricultural hinterland of villages: Holmwood, Beare Green, Newdigate, Capel and Ockley to the south; Brockham and Betchworth to the east; and Westcott, Wotton, Abinger, Coldharbour and Holmbury St Mary to the west. To the north lay the chalk escarpment of Box Hill and Ranmore, and the outlying villages of Pixham, Mickleham and Westhumble.

Pump Corner and South Street in the early twentieth century.

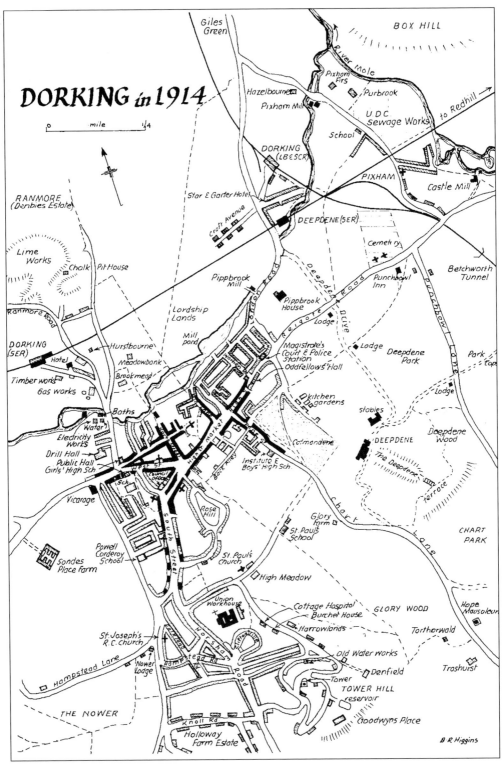

Map of Dorking in 1914, showing the new drill hall off West Street (now known as Drill Hall Road). (Map by Beryl Higgins, reproduced by permission of Dorking Local History Group)

Dorking High Street, 1914.

The surrounding area was primarily an agricultural one and much of what was consumed in Dorking was produced locally. The town provided for the needs of its hinterland with several water-driven mills on the River Mole and the Pippbrook, a forge and iron foundry, a coppersmith and ironmonger, more than one coach and car body workshop, and a timber merchant. It was served by two railway lines (the east-west South Eastern Railway (SER) line that ran between Reading and Redhill, and the north-south London to Brighton and South Coast Railway (LBSCR) line), and three stations. With an array of shops from agricultural feed stores to milliners and perfumers, Dorking was a thriving town, paved and gas-lit.

The area around the town was well-known, as it is today, for its hills and woods, particularly Leith Hill on the greensand to the south, and Box Hill on the chalk to the north. On warm summer weekends and bank holidays many thousands would come down from London, only 26 miles away, and alight at the town stations or at Holmwood to the south, to walk, picnic and take teas in the tea gardens, cafés and inns

Many recruitment speeches were made from the steps of the Red Lion Hotel in the High Street, shown here during the General Election of 1910.

Dorking High Street and Kingham's grocery, looking west towards Pump Corner, 1914.

St Martin's Church, Dorking in 1914.

A busy day on the High Street before the war.

Market animals in Dorking High Street before the war.

Visitors to Box Hill, 1914. (Image reproduced courtesy of the London Transport Museum)

Visitors to Leith Hill tower. In the summer of 1914 the tower counted Germans and Austrians among those who climbed for the views towards London and the south coast.

Lord Baden-Powell at a Scout rally at Ranmore, Whit Monday, 1914.

Dorking Fair in 1908. By 1914 the boys photographed would have been old enough to enlist.

that lined the roads towards the stations. Dorking had long been known for its cycle camps, which brought hundreds from London to camp at the foot of Box Hill each summer in a tented village that attracted thousands of day visitors to its events and processions. Lord Baden-Powell had attended a Boy Scout rally at Ranmore in the spring of 1914, and only months before the outbreak of war the financier Leopold Salomons of the nearby mansion at Norbury Park had bought Box Hill (which had been threatened with development), and given it to the nation, securing the town's importance as a leisure destination. Also popular were the open spaces of the Glory Wood, Betchworth Park with its golf course, and the Nower. The gloriously hot summer of 1914 saw visitors to the tower on top of Leith Hill from Canada, France, Denmark, Scotland, Ireland, Holland, Switzerland and, their plans made long before the crisis unfolding in that June and July, from Austria and Germany.

> ## DORKING and BOX HILL.
>
> DORKING is a delightfully situated town, on the old Roman road Stor.: Street, and was, during the Middle Ages, a stopping place of son importance on the road to London from the South Coast. It is pleasant seated in a valley of the river Mole on the southern slope of the North Down and has a station on the South Eastern and Chatham Railway and another the London, Brighton and South Coast Railway. There are many g residences in the neighbourhood, including Deepdene, situated in a beauti estate. Box Hill station, on the South Eastern and Chatham Railway, is at northern extremity of the town; the hill, which derives its name from the trees with which it is thickly covered, is about a mile from Dorking, and much frequented by picnic parties during the summer. Fares from Lon Bridge or Victoria (L.B. & S C. Railway) and Charing Cross, Cannon Str and London Bridge (S.E. & C. Railway): Single—1st Class, 4/-; *2nd Cla 2,6; 3rd Class, 2 . Return—1st Class, 6 ; *2nd Class, 4/6; 3rd Class. 3
> * Second Class fares by South Eastern & Chatham Railway only.
>
> ### HOUSE & ESTATE AGENTS.
> Frederick Arnold & Son, 12, High Street, Dorking. List on application.
> A. H. Lyne & Co., Dorking (adjoining L.B. & S.C, Ry. and close to Box H S.E. Ry. Stations.)
> White & Sons, F.S.I., House and Land Agents, Auctioneers and Val Dorking and Leatherhead.

The entry for Dorking in Kelly's Directory of spas and holiday destinations. Before the war – and after it – Dorking was a popular destination for day-trippers and holidaymakers. Thousands of people came down by bicycle, omnibus, train and private car on sunny weekends and bank holidays to walk and picnic on Box Hill and Leith Hill. The town produced its own mineral waters and ginger beers, and roadside houses and cottages operated as B&B accommodation and tea shops in the summer months.

The beauties of the hills had attracted the wealthy from London for many decades and a clutch of fine mansions surrounded the town, among them Deepdene, (once home to the art connoisseur, Thomas Hope, and now owned by the Duke of Newcastle), with its Italianate architecture and magnificent sculpture collection; Wotton House, home of the Evelyn family; Bury Hill, for a century the home of the Barclay brewing family; and Denbies, built by the Victorian master-builder, Thomas Cubitt, and now home to his son, George, the first Lord Ashcombe. In 1914 Lord Ashcombe's son, the Honourable Henry Cubitt, was Lord Lieutenant of Surrey. Among the eminent families living in substantial houses in and around the town were the

Deepdene, owned by the Duke of Newcastle, had been let before the war to tenants such as the Dowager Duchess of Marlborough. From 1915 members of the Surrey Yeomanry were stationed at the grand mansion on the edge of town. It never returned to residential use after the war.

Bury Hill, Westcott, home of the Barclay family. Troops trained in the grounds during the war.

Denbies, the home of Lord Ashcombe, whose son, Henry Cubitt, was Lord Lieutenant of Surrey in 1914.

Wedgwood-Vaughan Williams family of Leith Hill Place near Coldharbour; the Broadwood piano manufacturers of Lyne House in Capel; the Lloyd's insurance magnate Cuthbert Heath of Anstie Grange near Coldharbour; and Lord Farrer at Abinger Hall. When war broke out the inhabitants of these mansions, who controlled much of the land use, provided much of the funds for local initiatives and were large employers of local labour, would play a significant part in determining the town's response to the crisis.

In the town centre, along the roads to Reigate and Guildford, Leatherhead and Horsham and out in the villages were the villas of the town's successful traders, and of retired civil servants, bankers, colonial officials and ex-military men. Their inhabitants formed the committees and councils that ran towns and villages. Dorking was governed by the Dorking Urban District Council and the outlying areas of Holmwood and Westcott by the Dorking Rural District Council. Parish councils attended to business in the villages.

Politically the town was conservative in outlook on the major issues of the day. Imperial clubs flourished. Patrician locals provided respite accommodation to impoverished Londoners in holiday homes, or established local nursing schemes (such as Bertha Broadwood's Holt-Ockley method) to provide basic community health care, rather than seeking radical means to address poverty and inequality. The town also had active branches of the National League for Opposing Women's Suffrage and the Women's Anti-Suffrage League. However, there were dissenting voices. With three railway stations and goods yards in the town, Dorking had a vocal branch of the National Union of Railwaymen. In Newdigate socialists had set up holiday camps that were used by the London labour movement, and support for women's suffrage was strong, sometimes to the point of militancy. (In 1913 one of the greens of the newly-established Betchworth Park Golf Club was vandalized when V and W – representing Votes for Women – were carved into the turf.)

Church and community organizations flourished in the town and villages: the Band of Hope and the Church Army, the Oddfellows and the Ancient Order of Foresters, football and cricket leagues, cycling, rifle-shooting and athletic clubs, and volunteer fire brigades. On every occasion of national significance, such as a coronation or jubilee, the town band led processions of fancy dress participants and decorated

Children of the Dorking British School celebrating May Day, 1914. In the following years the war is an unspoken presence at May Day events, with Union flags and national colours on display.

B' S' MAY FESTIVAL 1914.
MAY POLE DANCERS.

Dorking Cricket Club at Pixham, 1912. The club abandoned all fixtures in the autumn of 1914, but every now and then throughout the war a team would be put together to play visiting soldiers or hospital teams.

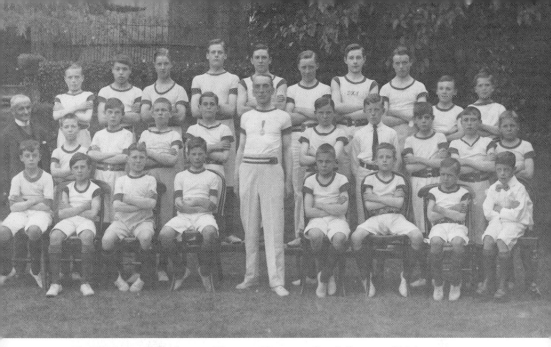

The Wesleyan gym class at Wyngate House on South Street, c.1914.

Dorking Fire Brigade outside the Fire Station at the Public Halls on West Street.

A decorated wagon depicting Britannia, her navy and her various colonies taking part in a procession through the town for the coronation of George V in 1911.

The Coronation Parade in Dorking High Street to celebrate the coronation of King George V in 1911.

The bonfire on Leith Hill to mark the coronation of King George V in 1911.

wagons through a High Street decked with Union flags and red, white and blue bunting.

There was a greater military presence in everyday life in the Britain of 1914 than is the case today and many in the town had military connections or regularly participated in some form of military activity. Since the unification of Germany in the 1860s (and in particular with the defeat of France in the Franco-Prussian War of 1871 which saw Alsace and Lorraine ceded from France to Germany), British governments had been nervous of the threat to the European balance of power from this new nation and of potential threats to the Empire. These concerns were conveyed to the British general public in an anonymously-written book published in 1871. *The Battle of Dorking* posited a future where Germany had defeated France and Holland and now looked to invade Britain. In a plausible scenario, the decisive battle to prevent the German army reaching London is fought at Dorking, where the Dorking gap in the chalk hills of the North Downs allows passage north to the capital. With Britain defeated and its Empire lost, the book provided a dire warning of the consequences of failing to take the German threat seriously. *The Battle of Dorking* was a huge seller, awakening public consciousness to the potential threat. Shortly after the publication of the book, forts were erected on Box Hill and Ranmore.

Locally George Cubitt (who by 1914 had become the first Lord Ashcombe), had responded by providing the local volunteer force with land and funds for a drill hall just off West Street. During the Boer War, civilians had been encouraged to take up rifle-shooting and the Dorking and District Rifle Club was formed. Using a small range at the drill hall, it was one of the first to be affiliated to the National Rifle Association. In 1901 Henry Lee-Steere of Jayes Park near Ockley provided an alternative two-target range at the foot of Bore Hill on Coldharbour Lane, and several of the mansions installed their own ranges.

By the early twentieth century, tensions in European relations meant that the threat of war in Europe was a growing concern, and Britain was not prepared for a war on land. Both France and Germany had universal male conscription, while Britain relied on a small professional regular army, which spent much of its time policing the colonies, and a large navy. This meant that it was up to local people to organize recruitment to territorial units, which would form a defence

Dorking Rifle Club, 1909. Rifle clubs were encouraged in towns and villages as local authorities anticipated calling on the citizenry to defend the country. When war broke out the High Sheriff of Surrey, Loe Strachey, encouraged rifle clubs to recruit and train and suggested that they be used to form guards in the villages in the event of invasion.

The Surrey Yeoman Inn on the High Street, named after the local yeomanry.

force and relieve the regular army by undertaking duties in the colonies should war break out and troops be needed in Europe. Without conscription, recruitment was ad hoc and locally-organized and, like most towns, Dorking had a small company of territorials. In 1908 the Surrey Territorial Force Association (chaired by the Lord Lieutenant) asked for assistance in recruiting local men. As a result, the Dorking Recruiting Committee was formed.

The following year the Surrey Territorial Force Association turned its attention to reservists. A company of the Surrey Veteran Reserve was formed, creating a register of trained men who had served in a branch of the armed forces for at least three years, or who had been on active service. Following a march of reservists at Horse Guards in London in June 1910, an appeal for men to come forward to join the Surrey companies brought a response from 270 men in the Dorking area. The Dorking Reserve Company was led by retired Colonel J.H. Verschoyle, assisted by Major Harman Young and Captain Touche.

By 1913 war in Europe was thought by many to be a probability. With Germany allied to Austria and France to Russia, a threat to any of the four nations might give rise to the spark that caused the conflagration, bringing alliances into play. Tensions had been bubbling in the Balkans – where Russia, Austria and Italy all had interests – for

The Surrey Yeomanry accompanying Princess Henry of Battenberg on a visit to Dorking on 1 June 1914. Degenhardt's store can be seen in the background.

decades. Awareness of the complex and delicate situation in the Balkans in particular was brought home to Dorking at New Year 1913 after peace delegates from the London Peace Conference of 1912–13 had witnessed the traditional Boxing Day hunt at the Burford Bridge Hotel at the foot of Box Hill. Convened at the end of the First Balkan War, the London conference sought to settle territorial claims after the successes of the Balkan armies in defeating the Ottoman Empire. Delegates attended from the six major powers (Britain, France, Italy, Russia, Germany and Austria-Hungary), as well as the smaller nations, all in pursuit of their own territorial and diplomatic aims. The Bulgarian and Serbian delegates and the Norwegian minister stayed with Cuthbert Heath at Anstie Grange and the local paper carried large photographs of the distinguished visitors as they met with the great and the good of the area, including Lord and Lady Farrer and Alfred Gwynne Vanderbilt (the American millionaire who was to die on the *Lusitania*).

The feeling that war was a possibility was pervasive. In 1913 Voluntary Aid Detachments were formed locally under the supervision of the Red Cross so that 'in the event of war in home territory an organised body can be relied upon to deal with the wounded in a skilled

manner'. The detachments were split into male and female divisions; the men requiring first-aid certificates, the women home nursing certificates. Even schools were prepared: the Dorking High School cadet force conducted field exercises and attended field days with the Surrey Secondary School Corps, and school magazines and end-of-year reports reproduced poems on military morale and praised the military virtues of duty and sacrifice.

Although the territorials had been drilling and tensions in Europe were running high, few would have expected the assassination of Archduke Franz Ferdinand, heir to the Emperor of Austria, in Sarajevo, Serbia, on 28 June 1914, to have an impact on Dorking. The local press made little comment when Austria, supported by its German ally, made demands for compensation and control over Serbia, or when Serbia conceded to most of the demands, save those that would undermine its independence. However, in early July the *Dorking and Leatherhead Advertiser* reported on the 'grim grey almost interminable line of warships that passed the Royal Standard' as the Royal Navy put to sea on review in a demonstration of power when, as the editorial asserted: 'we were never more anxious for peace.'

Dorking was enjoying an unusually warm summer when Austria announced war with Serbia on 25 July. The *Dorking and Leatherhead Advertiser* regretted the situation, finding it too absurd to be true that 'the murder of a prince by a fanatic... should send Europe in flames'. However, the editor concluded hopefully, there was no need to be alarmist, for 'the Emperor of Germany is a strong man, though he is peaceful'. The Kaiser, asserted the editorial, knew the horrors of war and diplomacy was being powerfully used. Nonetheless, he admitted to uncertainty: 'for England to be drawn into it must of course mean sacrifice to the masses of people, and in a larger measure perhaps than ever known.' Even so, he managed to turn the prospect of war into something positive. 'War yields us into a unity, as peace never does, and if ever there was a time when we needed Empire to mean more, and petty interest less, it is surely today,' he wrote, concluding that the war cloud might yet prove to be the hand of benediction.

As Russia backed Serbia, Germany took the side of Austria, declaring war on Russia on 1 August. Dorking, however, was awaiting the arrival in town of Bronco Bill's 'Great Wild West Exhibition and Mammoth Two-Ring Circus' on the Cotmandene. Its cowboys and

cowgirls, Indians, mustangs and lasso artists were expected in town on Thursday, 6 August. The Cinema Royal in the High Street was vying to outdo the Wild West Exhibition (or at least to capitalize on interest in it) by showing a film of the rival 'Buffalo Bill's Wild West Show' for three days while Bronco Bill was in town.

In the last week of peace, traditional summer holiday events proceeded as usual. The paper carried adverts for steamers to Southend and Margate. Local Boy Scouts went to camp at Southwick and marched to Worthing. A successful Hospital Saturday saw a decorated motor lorry encouraging collections for the cottage hospital in the villages, in pubs and in the streets. The Reverend William Russell Finlay entertained the Dorking Imperial Club, the Alexandra Club (which was the club's women's section), and the Junior Imperial Club to tea at Ribblesdale where the town band played in beautiful weather as the public strolled the gardens. At Betchworth Park golf course the final round of the annual cup was played. The

FIRST VISIT TO THIS COUNTRY.

BRONCHO BILL'S
GREAT
WILD WEST
EXHIBITION
AND MAMMOTH
TWO-RING CIRCUS
will positively visit
THE DENE, DORKING,
THURSDAY, AUGUST 6, 1914

FOR ONE DAY ONLY!

Nothing ever seen like this Gigantic Show in England Before!

THE REAL THING!
You have seen the Pictures of the Great Wild West.
Come and See the Reality!

COWBOYS AND COWGIRLS.
INDIANS! PRAIRIE MUSTANGS!
The World's Champion
LASSOO THROWERS.

BRONCHO BUSTERS
BREATH-TAKING LOG-CHARIOT RACING by Backwoodsmen.

THE GREAT SPECTACLE
The Attack on the Deadwood Coach, in which over
50 HORSES, COWBOYS, INDIANS 150 Etc., appear at one time.

In addition to our Wild West Exhibition we present our
GREAT CIRCUS SHOW
in Two Gigantic Rings, all should see
THE GREAT AERIAL BEKETOW TROUPE
in their marvellous performance on their high revolving Trapeze and Ladder. Nothing ever seen like this in a travelling concern before.

PRAIRIE BOB'S Great COWBOY BAND!

TWO EXHIBITIONS DAILY
Rain or Shine), at 3 and 8. Doors open 2.15 and 7.15. Seating Accommodation for 10,000.

Prices of Admission: 5s., 4s., 3s., 2s., 1s. and 6d. Children admitted to 3 o'clock Exhibition only at Half-price to all Seats. Eight o'clock Exhibition. Children Half-price except to 6d. Seats.

Seats may be booked and Plan seen at T. H. Smith and Sons, 16, High-street, Dorking.

The whole of the Entertainments will take place under one of the Largest Tents ever erected—
A VERITABLE TOWN OF CANVAS.

CINEMA ROYAL
HIGH STREET, DORKING.

MONDAY, TUESDAY AND WEDNESDAY NEXT.

BUFFALO BILL'S
WILD WEST SHOW

As performed at the Olympia, London, and before all the Crowned Heads of Europe. Buffalo Bill (Colonel Cody) himself in this picture. Over 1,000 performers. A complete moving picture representation, showing the Indians, Cowboys, Mexican Vaqueros, Russian Cossacks, Riders of all Nations, Queer Tribes and Performers from the Far East, Arabs and their famous Steeds, Japanese, Burmese, Cingalese, and strange inhabitants from many climes and countries, the Attack by Savages upon the Deadwood Stage Coach, the Burning of a Western Settler's Cabin, Thrilling Scenes of Adventure, illustrating the Wild Life of the Plains, the last great West, Elephants, Camels, and so forth.

BUFFALO BILL (HIMSELF),
The World's Champion Scout and Rifle Shot, shown in a series of Moving Pictures.

IN THREE ACTS at 3 o'clock and 8.10.

KINDLY NOTE.—To avoid disappointment in seeing this great picture, the Theatre opens every afternoon at 3 p.m.

Advert from the Dorking and Leatherhead Advertiser, 25 July 1914, for 'Bronco Bill's Great Wild West Exhibition and Mammoth Two-Ring Circus' on the Cotmandene. The show was due to open on 6 August, by which time war had been declared.

The Cinema Royal in the High Street sought to compete with the arrival of 'Bronco Bill's' by showing a film of rival 'Buffalo Bill's Wild West Show'.

Dorking branch of the National League for Opposing Women's Suffrage met at the mansion at High Ashurst on Box Hill where Lady Margaret Ryder opened her grounds to 150 people. Dorking and Woking police teams played a cricket match at Pixham Lane. The Rifle Club held its annual cup event. The Dorking Whippet Club took part in races at Eastbourne. Mickleham, Westcott, Wotton and Betchworth held their annual horticultural and produce shows. In addition, a Russian who had attempted suicide while staying at the Cudworth holiday camp near Newdigate was committed for trial.

On Bank Holiday Monday, 3 August, over 300 entries, many from outside the district, were received for the town's annual athletic sports meeting which was known as one of the best for 'flat' and cycling events in the national calendar. On the same day, Germany declared war on France. Because of the Franco-Russian alliance, any attack on Russia would amount to an attack

In the week before war broke out Reverend William Russell Finlay hosted a garden party for the Dorking Imperial Clubs. He was a great supporter of the Empire. On the outbreak of war he campaigned to prevent price rises caused by panic buying.

As German forces marched into Belgium on 3 August 1914, the Dorking and District Whippet Racing Association was racing its dogs at the bank holiday races in Eastbourne.

The Old Paulonians' Cycle Club, 1914. Dorking's St Paul's School had a reputation for athletic and cycling prowess at the annual Athletic Sports.

on France (who in any event had her eyes on regaining Alsace and Lorraine), so Germany moved to put France out of action. Germany demanded passage through Belgium for its troops, but Belgian independence and neutrality were guaranteed by the 1839 Treaty of London, by which all the signatory nations, including Britain, recognized the existence of the new and strategic state. German Chancellor von Hollweg claimed to find it inconceivable that Britain would go to war over this 'scrap of paper'.

Although Belgian neutrality was ostensibly the cause of war, there was more at stake for Britain than principle. The Belgian channel ports were vital to British trade with continental Europe, and a shift in the balance of power in

Dorking's annual Athletic Sports were held on the bank holiday, 3 August, the day before war was declared.

Europe with a triumphant Germany and a defeated France – and possibly Russia – might see greater threats to Britain itself and to the Empire. The British fleet prepared to put to sea and the army was mobilized. The *Surrey Advertiser* of 5 August, which went to press before war had finally been declared, reported that 'Interest at Dorking, Leatherhead and Epsom is at fever heat with regard to the crisis in Europe – especially as many men in all three places are reservists.' However, the athletics went ahead on the bank holiday with the town band in attendance.

Within days the same band would be playing the territorials off at the station and touring the villages to recruit volunteers.

The Dorking Town Band, c.1914. The band played at all town events, from coronation processions and jubilees to village fêtes and church parades. On the outbreak of war it played troops off at the station and toured the villages with the recruitment committee.

The Battle of Dorking

The fictional account of a decisive battle at Dorking took place in 1875, almost forty years before the possibility became a real fear in 1914. Germany had defeated France and annexed Holland and Denmark. Britain declared war and Germany invaded an ill-prepared nation. German troops came ashore at Worthing and began moving inland.

Written by Sir George Chesney, *The Battle of Dorking* was published anonymously in *Blackwood's Magazine* in 1871. In

Chesney's tale, a battle takes place at Dorking between the invaders and British defenders; Dorking occupies a strategically vital point between the troops' landing-point on the south coast and London. Failure to defend the heights of Ranmore and Box Hill on each side of the Mole Gap allows the invaders to pass through to London. Britain is left humiliated, its Empire lost.

The story caught the public imagination. When reprinted it sold 80,000 copies and was translated into a score of languages. There was no immediate military response but in the 1880s forts were erected on Box Hill and Ranmore, and George

The front cover of The Battle of Dorking, 1871.

Cubitt (later Lord Ashcombe), owner of Denbies, provided the local volunteer force with land and funds for a drill hall in the town.

When the book was written Germany had only recently emerged as a unified nation, on the amalgamation of German-speaking states and territories. The book is a manifestation of fear of a unified Germany and its likely military aggression. Although its notoriety arose from the concerns of its time – the birth of a unified Germany, the unfitness of the British army, and the development of new means of transport and communication – the tale had a long life in public consciousness in both Britain and Germany. In the 1940s a German edition was issued to Hitler's army under the title *Was England Erwartet* (*What England Expects*).

CHAPTER 2

1914: Recall and Recruitment

When Britain declared war on Germany on Tuesday, 4 August 1914 Canon Palmes at St Mary Magdalene, South Holmwood, announced that a bell would toll at 12 noon each day for the duration of hostilities. He asked that those who heard it might lift their hearts to God for the sake of those serving at the front.

Captain W.L. Hodges, commanding officer of the Dorking Company of Territorials in 1914.

The first indication that the threat of war had become reality was the recall of reservists and the mobilization of territorials. Crowds gathered at Dorking Post Office when the notice went up recalling all reservists. Among those recalled were four policemen, two Urban District Council workmen and a postman. Post Office staff struggled with the number of telegrams and letters containing mobilization orders, large numbers gathered to read incoming communications, and when the ultimatum to the Kaiser expired the crowd sang patriotic songs in the High Street.

The Dorking Company of the 5th Battalion the Queen's (Royal West Surrey) Regiment was at its annual training camp near Salisbury when the orders went out. The Queen's were territorials, part-time soldiers who had signed up to undertake duties at home and in the Empire in the event of war. Their deployment would enable units of

In the early days of the war Dorking boy scouts were at camp on the Sussex coast and they made themselves useful by giving assistance to HM Coastguard.

The Dorking Company of the 5th Battalion the Queen's (Royal West Surrey) Regiment leaving Dorking South Eastern Railway Station (now known as Dorking West) after mobilization,

the regular army, which were policing the colonies, to be brought back to fight in France. 'G' Company was based in Dorking and trained at the drill hall; it also had detachments that drilled in Holmwood and Shere. The company recruited from Dorking, Abinger, Betchworth, Capel, Coldharbour, Gomshall, Holmwood, Newdigate, Ockley, Peaslake, Ranmore, Shere, Westcott and Wotton. Men from the Brockham area drilled with 'A' (Reigate) Company.

Camp was broken and the company was sent back to mobilize, arriving in Dorking at 10pm on the night of 4 August. At 10am the next morning ninety-nine men mustered for medical inspection at the drill hall. After inspection they were addressed by Canon Chichester of St Martin's and Henry Cubitt, who told them that they were envied by those staying behind. 'Are we downhearted?' Cubitt asked them. 'Are we afraid of the Germans?' The men then marched to the

Canon Chichester of St Martin's Church, Dorking, was brother-in-law to Henry Cubitt, Lord Lieutenant of Surrey.

South Eastern Railway station, accompanied by the town band. Cheering crowds lined the road and 2,000 people watched from the platforms or from the banks alongside the railway tracks as the men embarked on a special troop train for Strood camp near Chatham while the band played *Auld Lang Syne*, *Rule Britannia* and the national anthem. Twelve recruits were inspired to join up during the course of the day. The Queen's formed part of the Surrey Infantry Brigade of the

Henry Cubitt was the son of George Cubitt (the first Lord Ashcombe), and grandson of the master builder Thomas Cubitt. Educated at Eton and Trinity College, Cambridge, Henry Cubitt had been a Conservative Member of Parliament between 1892 and 1906 and was Lord Lieutenant of Surrey when war broke out. He lived at Birtley Court in Bramley near Guildford, but had strong connections with the Cubitt family home at Denbies and was an energetic recruiter in the Dorking district. He succeeded to his father's title and inherited Denbies in 1917, becoming the second Lord Ashcombe. A keen recruiter locally, he lost his three eldest sons to the war.

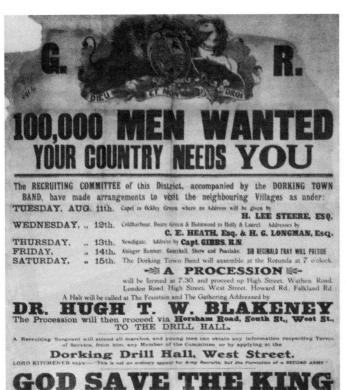

Mr Pardon-Howe, leader of Dorking Urban District Council in 1914.

Poster for a recruiting week in Dorking and the villages, August 1914. (Photo courtesy of Roy Williamson)

Home Counties Division and was eventually sent out to India.

So quickly were reservists (those who had served in the regular army but who were committed to remain in reserve for a number of years after discharge) recalled that employers had no notice of their imminent departure. Council employees left having been paid their wages in advance but with three days' work unperformed. The Council resolved to keep the men's positions open for them when released from mobilization and to allow them to treat the monies overpaid as holiday pay.

Recruitment began immediately. Compared to France and Germany, Britain had only a small regular army, traditionally having relied on the Royal Navy for defence. The regular army was generally employed as an order-keeping force in the colonies rather than for fighting continental wars, so if Britain was to be effective the British army

would need to be enlarged. However, unlike France and Germany where every man was required to serve in the army for a period, Britain relied on voluntary enlistment; hence there was no large pool of trained men to call on. In the early days of August 1914 Secretary of State for War Lord Kitchener called for 100,000 volunteers to form a new army. The local recruiting committee immediately arranged a series of recruitment meetings. Posters 5 feet high in red lettering advertised the recruitment party's progress through the town and villages with the town band playing them on their way. On Tuesday 11 August it progressed from Capel to Ockley where the crowd was addressed by Henry Lee-Steere of nearby Jayes Park. (Mr Lee-Steere was to lose his only child, 19-year-old Lieutenant John Henry Lee-Steere, within three months.)

The following day the party made its way from Coldharbour, via Beare Green, to the Holly and Laurel at South Holmwood where Cuthbert Heath of Anstie Grange and H.G. Longman (Holmwood resident and member of the Longman publishing family) spoke. Captain Alfred Gibbs of the Royal Navy (who lived at Hillview) spoke

Henry Lee-Steere JP of Jayes Park (pictured here on the right with his young son, John, in about 1900) spoke at recruitment rallies at nearby Ockley. John was killed in action before the end of the year. (Photo reproduced courtesy of Gordon Lee-Steere)

on the 13th at Newdigate, and Sir Reginald Bray, lord of the manor of Shere, presided at the recruiting drives at Abinger Hammer, Gomshall, Shere and Peaslake. The week's activities culminated on the evening of Saturday 15 August with a procession of recruits, accompanied by the town band, from the Rotunda on South Street through the streets of Dorking: up the High Street, down Wathen Road and into London Road, back into the High Street and into West Street, then into Howard Road and Falkland Road.

The procession halted at the fountain outside the Falkland Arms, where the gathering was addressed by Dr Hugh T.W. Blakeney who said that England and the Empire were in a perilous position and that the local recruiting committee was toiling hard to bring in recruits. It was, he said, a pleasure to do so, and he reported that the call had met with an excellent response in a glorious way: some 100 men had been

Dr Hugh Blakeney, who led the August 1914 recruiting campaign.

The Falkland Arms and the fountain (demolished as a hazard in the blackout in the Second World War), where recruiting rallies addressed crowds in the autumn of 1914.

The Red Lion Hotel on the High Street from whose steps recruitment campaigners spoke to farmers at the market and crowds during recruitment rallies.

enrolled in Dorking for the new army. The party then progressed from the Horsham Road up South Street. At the Red Lion Dr Blakeney spoke to hundreds and the band played the national anthems of Belgium, France, Russia and Great Britain before the procession continued via West Street to the drill hall. The local paper reported that the event brought Dorking's enlistment figures to eighty for the regular army and thirty-one for the territorials. Not everyone, however, was enthusiastic: local Quakers put up posters calling for peace (two of which were torn down by a recruiting officer), and when Cuthbert Heath spoke in Holmwood he was heckled by a drunk.

Men from all backgrounds joined up in the early days of the war. Some were driven by patriotism or disgust at tales of murdered Belgian civilians and desecrated churches in the press. Others were attracted by the prospect of a regular wage and a full belly, or by the chance to see something of the world. Some even returned from parts of the Empire, with their families being left to live with other family members. Harold Pethick, whose sister was the suffragette campaigner Emmeline Pethick-Lawrence, returned from Canada with his wife Evie to enlist; when he went to war Evie remained with Emmeline in

Dorking livestock market in the High Street. It was at the weekly market that Henry Cubitt exhorted local farmers to persuade their labourers in outlying areas to join up.

Holmwood. Gerard Theodore Bray also returned to England from Canada with his wife, Evelyn Joan nee Broadwood, so that he could enlist; Mrs Bray and her children returned to the Broadwood family fold to live with her sister Audrey Innes at The Greenings near Charlwood. (Second Lieutenant Bray was killed within twenty-four hours of landing at Gallipoli in August 1915.) Newly-married reservist George Henry Ackland from Newdigate was working as a policeman in Fremantle, Western Australia, when he was recalled to his regiment.

After the first wave of enthusiasm, encouragement to enlist was required and Henry Cubitt attended Dorking market at the end of August to address the farmers gathered there. Speaking from the steps of the Red Lion Hotel, he said that he had recruited widely in Dorking and the villages but wanted to reach the outlying agricultural areas. He

asked employers to impress upon young men the need to join up and announced that he had informed all his employees at Denbies that there would not be as much work going in future and it would be married men who would be given first consideration for available work. With such moves common among many employers, single men often faced a choice: join up or face unemployment.

The local paper kept up calls for recruits and printed rousing patriotic calls to arms, sometimes in poetic form. Further recruitment meetings were held in Leigh, in the school playground at Capel, and at the cricket ground in Holmwood, but Cubitt was disappointed by the number of townsmen and villagers coming forward. He announced in the *Surrey Advertiser* that in order to encourage enlistment, he and 'the principal people' of Dorking district were signing a pledge that at

Lord Ashcombe, father of Henry Cubitt and owner of the Denbies estate and farms in 1914.

Two poems, both titled A Call to Arms, were published in the Dorking and Leatherhead Advertiser in the autumn of 1914. Their style and tone are typical of recruitment poems that appeared regularly in the paper.

A CALL TO ARMS.

Once more the call to arms we hear,
The bugle notes are loud and clear;
And as each note thrills through the air,
It bids us to prepare, prepare!

Arm, arm, ye brave! Proud Albion's race
Have met the foemen face to face;
And on each ridge and rocky height
They storm the crest and win the fight.

The cannons' roar, the leaden hail
Cannot their martial ardour quail;
Brave Scots and Celts now show their might,
And drive the foe in headlong flight.

Colonial hearts beat true and strong,
Under the flag they proudly throng;
And hand in hand we sweep the main,
For naught can e'er our power restrain.

Charge! with a ringing cheer,
Charge! till the field is clear,
No one will falter.

G.

Dorking.

A CALL TO ARMS.

Awake young men of England, regard
your country's call,
We have been told by Kitchener that he
will want you all,
Keep the colours flying, we will not own
defeat,
Compel the German Emperor to kneel at
England's feet.
Avenge the plucky Belgians, who fought
bravely to defend,
Enlist to fight the foe, until this war is
at an end.
Come flocking by the thousands, we want
you every one,
We cannot rest contented, until this deed
is done.
Our brave Allies, the Russians, are vic-
torious with their work,
And you who are of British blood, your
duty must not shirk.
Forget not our French brothers, fighting
by us, for their sake-
We must drive back the enemy, our free-
dom is at stake.
Once more we do entreat you, enlist before too late,
Then soon the German Emperor shall
rightly know his fate.

A. T. SAUNDERS, Dorking.

the end of the war they would give preference in employment to those who had served. They hoped that this would encourage men to enlist. In an area where large landowners owned many farms and businesses, as well as employing scores in their mansions and gardens, fear of being denied future employment was potentially persuasive. Cubitt quoted one local landowner's success in sending his employees forward: 'I think you will be glad to hear that I have no longer a single man between 19 and 30 years old on my place, if all pass the doctor ten fine lads are joining Kitchener's Army from house, garage, garden and farm.'

Leopold Salomons of Norbury Park had given Box Hill to the nation in the spring of 1914. (Image reproduced by permission of The National Trust)

At a meeting at Mickleham Leopold Salomons of Norbury Park offered every unmarried man in his employment who joined Kitchener's Army half pay while he was away; married men would receive full pay with half going to their wives and entitlement to 5 acres of land for growing vegetables. At the end of August Salomons personally canvassed his staff to encourage them to come forward and fourteen of them enlisted. When, the following week, he advertised for replacement staff at Norbury Park, the paper carried a notice that men of army age need not apply as only younger or older men would be considered, or those unfit for military service. For those who did not enlist, not only was there the fear of no jobs in the future, but many jobs were thus barred to them immediately; this at a time when unemployment in the area was rising

MEN OF ARMY AGE NEED NOT APPLY.

A notice in our advertisement columns intimates that men are required at Norbury Park to replace those who have joined the Colours. The notice particularly applies to those who have been rejected as medically unfit for national service, and to men over 40 and boys under 18.

An announcement that men of military age need not apply for jobs at Norbury Park carried by the Dorking and Leatherhead Advertiser. Leopold Salomons was recruiting as he had persuaded a large number of his staff to enlist.

as planned projects were being shelved and employers were economizing in general.

A letter to the *Dorking and Leatherhead Advertiser* alleged that some employers were sacking men if they did not join up, whereupon they had no choice but to enlist. This was not a volunteer army, contended Charles Smith, but unrecognized conscription of employees by their employers. Such tactics by the well-to-do, alleged another correspondent, were causing much resentment among working people. If 'compulsory enlistment' was to be imposed, he suggested it ought to be by vote of the nation, not by individuals with the power to exert unfair pressure.

Even outside of employment, men were under pressure to explain why they had not joined up, and the High Sheriff of Surrey, Loe Strachey, decided that it was necessary to issue badges of gratitude to those who had tried to enlist but had been rejected for medical or height reasons, in order to identify them. The first such badges were issued in early October.

Letters to the paper allege that not all enlistment was voluntary, with men being thrown out of work by patriotic employers if they did not enlist. With many potential employers only taking on married or older men, many single working men were left with little alternative.

Some employers promoted enlistment by not offering jobs to men of military age, instead employing only married, under- or over-age men in order to encourage men of appropriate age to enlist.

HOW TO HINDER ENLISTING.

[To the Editor.]

Sir,—It has come to my knowledge that some employers are telling those whom they employ that they must either enlist or be discharged. This compulsion excites great resentment amongst the working classes, and will have a very bad effect. If we are to have compulsory enlistment let it be by the vote of the nation, and not by the unfair pressure of individuals. I believe these cases are not numerous, but it is well that those who take this course should know that they are doing more harm than good.—Yours, etc.,

ONE WHO KNOWS.

EMPLOYERS AND COMPULSORY ENLISTMENT.

[To the Editor.]

Sir,—In a previous issue you inserted a letter dealing with the prevalence of what is undoubtedly a real grievance in regard to the manner in which men are being compelled to enlist for active service on pain of dismissal by their employers.

These tales have been so persistent that I have been at pains to verify some of them, with the result that I am prepared to give, through the Editor of the ADVERTISER, the names of employers and employees in at least two cases.

In one case the man dismissed told me himself, and in another case the information comes from a source which forbids doubt.

In one case the man offered to enlist when the war first commenced but was prevented, only to be compelled later. In the other the man intimated that he did not wish to enlist, was dismissed, and being unable to obtain work has now joined the forces.

We cannot in these circumstances pride ourselves any longer on our voluntary Army.

I am sure men would much rather recognise conscription.—Yours, etc.,

CHAS. W. SMITH.
Dorking, Sept. 24th, 1914.

Some of those who responded to Lord Kitchener's call for volunteers might have better served the war effort at home. In September Mr Lay, the headmaster of South Holmwood School, announced that he was joining up and he was gone the next day. When conscription was introduced later in the war, his occupation would have been rated important enough for him to be exempted, at least initially. However, as a result of his departure the school got its first (temporary) female head teacher, Frances Morris. The same happened at Newdigate School: when the headmaster, John Steeds, was called up the school took on a certificated headmistress until his return. Kate Simpson and Bessie Bixby (daughter of Joseph Bixby, an earlier headmaster at South Holmwood School) both served in the role during the war. A stroke of bad timing also saw local schools deprived of the services of Leonard Roberts, who taught woodwork at St Paul's School and the Dorking British School. On holiday in Berlin when war broke out, he found himself marooned in Germany where he was interned throughout the war.

By early September the local paper estimated that Dorking had supplied 225 men to the new army and 53 had joined the territorials; the outlying district of Holmwood had seen 38 men leave the area (23 reservists and territorials and the rest newly-enlisted). On 19 September the *Dorking and Leatherhead Advertiser* carried a long list of names of those enlisted from Dorking and the villages; the list included seven brothers from the Mackrell family.

By the beginning of September the goalkeeper of Dorking's football

A DORKING RECORD.
" WE ARE SEVEN."

Seven brothers in the forces. We should say this is a record for a Dorking family. This distinction is held by the family of the late Mr. Robert Mackrell, who was for nearly 40 years a printer in the employ of the late Mr. Charles Rowe. With the exception of one (who is a gunner in the Royal Garrison Artillery), all are serving in the Royal Navy. Some were on active service previous to the outbreak of war; others were in the Reserve, and have been called up, and the remaining brothers have joined since. It will be interesting to hear if this record can be beaten, or how nearly approached.

The Dorking and Leatherhead Advertiser of 7 October 1914 relates that seven Dorking brothers were by then serving in the armed forces: Robert, William, Albert, Charles, Ernest, Percy and Frank Mackrell were the sons of Robert Mackrell, a retired printer who had worked for forty years at Rowe's in Dorking. Percy and Frank did not return.

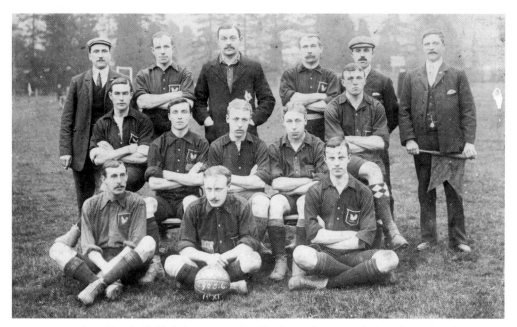

Dorking Football Club, known as 'the Chicks', a few years before the outbreak of war.

team, 'the Chicks', had been recalled for service. Otherwise, the town was fielding a full team. However, teams were coming under pressure to be seen to be supporting the war effort. Football was seen as a distraction for young men who ought to have been enlisting and there was national debate on the morality of professional football being played while the country was at war and a concerted campaign to shame professional players into enlisting. (Some teams – famously Edinburgh's Heart of Midlothian – answered the call by joining up en masse.) In late August, in the hope of avoiding criticism, a nervous Surrey County Football Association gave local teams a dispensation to continue to play matches, but only if all receipts went to the Prince of Wales' Relief Fund. However, by early September 'the Chicks' faced critical letters in the local paper suggesting that there ought not to be enough able-bodied young men left in Dorking to form a team. At a meeting at the Red Lion Hotel the club cancelled all its fixtures for the season, announcing that it would be unpatriotic and 'ungracious' to those who had enlisted to carry on playing and to give their places to those who had declined to enlist. The Cricket Club followed suit, followed by the Warnham Staghounds. In December the annual Boxing Day hunt meet at the Burford Bridge Hotel was also cancelled.

It was not just in the loss of men that the effects of war were immediately felt. The *Dorking and Leatherhead Advertiser* announced a reduction in paper size. Riding and carriage horses were commandeered for use by the army. (In 1914 nearly all military transport for supplies and artillery was pulled by horse.) Bus services were reduced as petrol was diverted to the military, and reservist East Surrey Traction Company employees were recalled for military service. Trees in Redlands Wood, between Holmwood and Coldharbour, were cut for pit-props and

Dorking Football club came under pressure to give up the season's fixtures when letters to the paper criticized players' patriotism, suggesting that there should be no young men left in the district to play football. In the same week, the team abandoned the league.

FOOTBALL AND THE WAR.

[To THE EDITOR.]

Sir,—I read with surprise and disgust in your issue of Saturday that the Dorking Football Club is making up its programme for the autumn. At a time like this, when England is fighting for everything we hold dear, there should be no young men left who can play football, and the clubs should realise what their plain duty is in the matter. There should be no prospect of "nearly all the old players being again available," as the bulk of them should have offered to help their country in her dire need. Do the young men not realise that our independence as a nation is at stake, that they can think of amusing themselves at this juncture? It is well to try and face the ordeal before us with courage and even cheerfulness, but no amusements of any kind should stand before a man's solemn duty to his country. The plain duty of the football clubs throughout the country is to try and induce their players to enlist in Lord Kitchener's Army, not to make plans for autumn matches. I have no male relations who are not already serving their King, and I think if the men of the town will not do it the women should endeavour to start a crusade against the selfish idea that people must amuse themselves, and the army can do the fighting. Before your next issue our heroic little army may be annihilated. Will you then be talking of matches?—Yours, etc.,

K. M. POWELL.

Goodwyns Place, Dorking, Aug. 30th, 1914.

[The Dorking Football Club has decided to cancel all their fixtures.—Ed.]

Mickleham volunteer fire brigade. As early as late 1914 the village of Mickleham was struggling to keep its fire brigade operational with the exodus of village men to the services, and boy scouts were seeking to fill the gap.

trench linings. The South Eastern Railway's Redhill to Reading line, with its two Dorking stations, saw troops and military freight passing from many points towards France. Private wirelesses had to be taken down and the Box Hill rifle range was closed to conserve ammunition (despite calls for ranges to remain open so that townspeople might train for the defence of their homes). The Urban District Council postponed the much-hoped-for acquisition of the Nower from the Barclay family of Bury Hill because of concerns that it would prove impossible to obtain a loan. Food and commodity prices rose as those who could afford it bought large stocks of goods for fear of future shortages, pushing prices out of the reach of those on more limited incomes. The Urban District Council appealed to the better-off to desist from buying more than they needed and some traders sought to ensure supplies for all by refusing to sell in bulk. Kinghams, the High Street grocers, offered the wives of reservists and territorials the chance to purchase supplies of groceries at pre-war prices on particular days, and employers had to advance wages to workers as prices had risen so much. Even so, traders struggled as nervous wholesalers refused to extend credit,

Price rises and withdrawal of credit hit Dorking's traders with the outbreak of war. The Chamber of Commerce appealed to people to support local traders in order to keep employees in work.

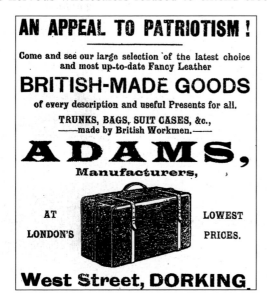

Adams & Co. of West Street, Dorking, make a direct appeal to patriotism in advertising their British-made bags and trunks.

demanding payment in cash for all supplies. Traders selling groceries on account (as was common practice) faced being unable to stock their stores until accounts were settled in cash. On 22 August the Chamber of Commerce took out a 'Patriotism notice' urging people to save jobs by supporting their local traders, and local artist George Gardiner wrote to the paper, urging people to pay for goods in cash rather than on account.

It was not only retail jobs that were under threat. Wealthy households cut back on indoor and outdoor staff, and construction works were cancelled or postponed until the situation was more settled. In a typical move, the Dorking British School announced that a gift for building works would be held in abeyance until such 'troublous times' had passed. A consequent rise in unemployment was a real fear for the councils and parishes as relief payments to those who were unable to feed, house and clothe themselves and their families – even as a direct result of the war – were the responsibility of local councils and parishes (and the local ratepayer) rather than central government. The Urban District Council urged employers to retain staff and not to put off planned building works. In September discussions began with Surrey County Council about the possibility of funding road-widening works at Westcott in order to keep unemployment down. However, by October nearly sixty men in the building trade were out of work and the Urban District Council was discussing proposals to provide work with local landowners.

In response, the Urban District Council formed a charitable relief committee to deal with calls for financial assistance from those affected by the war. It was immediately supported with a round of fund-raising. The village of Abinger followed the Urban District Council's lead and set up a committee to take in donations and to offer relief to those suffering financial hardship, a move that was followed by all the villages in the following months. Newdigate's emergency committee also took responsibility for recruiting and comprised members of the parish council, the clergy, and all the local clubs and societies. In Holmwood, where many found themselves short of work, the churchwardens decided to go ahead with plans to improve the church in the express hope of employing some of the labourers who had lost their jobs. The only positive economic news was that many wealthy people who would have gone abroad for their holidays in August chose

instead to come down to Dorking, and the Chamber of Commerce had to call for apartments and rooms to let to meet this need.

Nevertheless, councils and parishes soon had cause to fear that they would be responsible for even more hardship than anticipated, this time arising directly from military action. As news of disastrous losses in France and Belgium came through, councillors alarmed at the prospect of calls on ratepayers to fund welfare payments to the injured and the dependants of those killed or injured petitioned the prime minister, the Chancellor of the Exchequer, the Admiralty, the Secretary of State for War and local Members of Parliament, calling for government provision rather than that of hard-pressed local councils.

The British Expeditionary Force, under the command of Sir John French, had arrived in France on 17 August 1914. It was engaged by the Germans around the town of Mons on 23 August and Britain's 'contemptible little army' – as described by the Kaiser – was pushed back with heavy losses. Dorking district's first casualties were Arthur Frederick Curry of the Somerset Light Infantry who died on 26 August, just three weeks after the declaration of war, and James Mercer of Holmwood who died the following day. With rapid German advances through Belgium and northern France (before they were halted short of the English Channel in the 'Race to the Sea'), many members of the British Expeditionary Force found themselves cut off and taken prisoner. Private Alan Skett of the Coldstream Guards, whose parents were living at Royston Cottage in North Holmwood, was wounded in the legs at Mons. Taken prisoner, he eventually died in April 1917 on a route march when he was shot for falling out of the line through exhaustion.

Military news created animosity towards Germans resident in Britain and Mr Degenhardt of the prestigious store on South Street found himself the target of such abuse that he wrote to the newspaper asserting that, despite his name, he was in fact British-born and bred.

When news of the setbacks came through, many felt obliged to take up arms in their country's hour of need. In mid-October the town band played another contingent of reservists from the drill hall to the SER station. The following week the 5th Battalion The Queen's (Royal West Surrey) Regiment completed training and passed through Redhill, where many local people gathered on the platform to see them off.

Charles Degenhardt in later life. That Mr Degenhardt of the South Street store felt it necessary to announce in the paper that he was not German suggests that he had been the victim of abuse or harassment on account of his German name. There was suspicion about enemy aliens living locally. In early September a German maid named Dora Victoria Wickmann was arrested and charged with having breached the 5-mile restriction on movement imposed on her by the Alien Act when she was brought by her London employer to the family's country home at Frolbury at Felday, Abinger. In November the police announced that, in response to local concerns at foreigners allegedly having bought or rented houses in strategic positions on the hills, they had investigated each of them and found nothing of concern.

Recruiting continued throughout late summer and early autumn, and between October and December 1914 at least eighty ex-pupils from the Dorking British School alone enlisted. By December the Post Office announced that 56 per cent of its outdoor post staff was in the services, together with 33 per cent of the 'indoor' staff. Along with Henry Cubitt, Leopold Salomons and Dr Blakeney, Cuthbert Heath was one of the district's most committed recruiters. He gave pep talks at Anstie Grange to volunteers from his estates and from the villages of Holmwood and Coldharbour. His office at Lloyd's of London became a recruitment centre with attesting officers ready to swear in Lloyd's men wanting to join up. 'Our family is doing well,' recorded his daughter Genesta in late 1914, for her brother and all seven of her male cousins had enlisted.

Schools and parishes logged those who were serving in an ad hoc manner, printing lists of names in parish magazines and end-of-year

The Dorking Company of the Queen's (Royal West Surrey) Regiment serving in India.

reports. The Dorking British School printed a roll of honour of those known to be serving, listing sixty-four in the army and another sixteen in the Royal Navy. By the end of 1915, this had reached 156 in the army and 22 in the Royal Navy. Dorking High School estimated that some forty ex-pupils were serving by December 1914, including G.K. Rose, who had left mid-term to take up a commission in the Royal Field Artillery. He was reported to have been the envy of all. The Dorking British School's annual report commented confidently on the role of education in preparing boys for the challenges that they would face. In an article entitled 'Pro Patria', congratulations were extended to the nation's schools, the editor claiming that the rapid fitness attained by recruits was down to excellent physical training in schools. (In fact, a not insignificant proportion of men enlisting had to be rejected from service on being found to be in poor physical shape.) School curricula subtly changed to reflect the increasing military influence on society: at Dorking High School military drill replaced physical education, and at Mickleham School the end-of-year prize-giving saw infants demonstrating drill and reciting 'The Battle of Mons' and 'Little Tommy Atkins'. The Dorking British School journal editor praised schools for teaching pupils to understand the struggle between might and right, the importance of national and personal honour, of fidelity to promises made, and of protection of the weak. However, one former pupil, contacted in a drive to create a roll of honour, wrote to the headmaster of a more prosaic virtue learned in school:

> One has very little to do in hospital but read, write and think, and my mind has often gone back to the very happy days I spent at the dear old British School. I have often wondered how many soldiers have realised that it was at the School where they obtained (or at any rate where they ought to have obtained) that quality which is so essential to a soldier – obedience.

Dorking Urban District Council agreed to keep open the jobs of the reservists and territorials among its staff who had been called up. Initially it also resolved to pay them half their weekly wages, which they would receive in addition to their army pay (the money would be banked by the council surveyor for the men's wives if they were married). The following year, however, with no end to hostilities

anticipated, councillors thought better of the offer, especially when it was discovered that some of the men were being paid more than they had previously earned in the employ of the council. It was resolved to keep the men's positions open to them – as did local schools for serving masters – but to restrict the part-payments of salary to a year.

In early October the first list of the wounded appeared in the *Surrey Advertiser* and the *Dorking and Leatherhead Advertiser*. The First Battle of Ypres, between October and November 1914, saw over 300 missing or wounded from the East Surrey Regiment alone, and it claimed nine lives from the town. The first long casualty list appeared in the *Dorking and Leatherhead Advertiser* on 24 October and the first obituary for a local man killed in action on 21 November. Reservist Albert Reader, a relief porter at Dorking Station until his recall, had died a month earlier at Ypres. Subsequent November and December editions carried lists of those wounded or missing at the First Battle of Ypres, and a slow trickle of deaths in action. Perhaps it was heightened awareness of these deaths and a wish to show respect for all whose deaths were being reported that prompted a high turnout for the funeral of Edward Taylor at Dorking Cemetery in late December. A reservist postman who had covered rounds in Capel and Newdigate, Dorking, Westcott and Mickleham, Taylor was hit by a train while guarding a

Two embroidered cards sent back to Dorking from troops serving with the British Expeditionary Force.

bridge at Woking Junction and died of his injuries. Huge crowds turned out to watch his funeral cortège pass from Falkland Road to the cemetery where the town band played *The Funeral March* as the coffin, draped in a Union flag, was borne in by members of the Surrey Yeomanry. Full military honours were accorded him; three volleys were fired by his colleagues, and buglers sounded *The Last Post*.

News of conditions in France and Belgium slowly trickled back by way of letters; many of these, despite their negative content, were printed in the local paper. Bernard Curtis, who was driving a motor ambulance in a part of France that reminded him of Box Hill, wrote of the lies that had encouraged men to join up. Private Len Matthews, previously groundsman at Dorking Golf Club, told of his time living in turnip fields in a piece headlined 'Too awful for words'.

News of German successes in France turned official thoughts to the possibility, inconceivable in the optimism of early August, of war on British soil. In November a local defence committee was set up under the Defence of the Realm Act 1914 (DORA). Sub-committees were formed to take responsibility for the defence of the villages and outlying areas. The Dorking Defence Committee's first task was to compile a list of all horses, cattle and sheep in the area, and of cars and motorcycles, so that plans might be made for the evacuation of anything that might be of assistance to the Kaiser's armies should the country be invaded. Eighty-six special constables (many of them, according to the *Dorking and Leatherhead Advertiser*, 'well-to-do') had been appointed in early August; more were now appointed to enforce the decisions of the committees in the expectation of reluctance to cooperate, or even outright resistance, from some of the local

---

A REMINDER OF BOX HILL.

Bernard A. Curtis, chauffeur of a motor ambulance, writes from the scene of the war:—

I went with a convoy of ambulances to a place which reminded me of Box Hill. On the side of the hill was a pretty little house like the one which Meredith lived in. I was sent back with a few German wounded, and not one was over 20 years of age.

One of the wounded told me a pitiful story. He said he had been at a school at Margate, and had only received six weeks' training when he was sent into the fighting line. He had been told that Calais was in the hands of the Germans, and that we had lost nearly all our fleet.

When I told them it was all lies one of them got excited and said, "We have been deceived; we have been told lies." They also told me that their corps had been inspected by the Kaiser before they were sent off, who said that his troops were meeting with success in all quarters, and that the British were worn out and could not hold out much longer.

The poor fellow was badly wounded, and he gave me the name and address of a young lady in England, and asked me to write and tell her he had died for his country, and that he hoped she would have kind thoughts for him. Before we got to the hospital he was dead.

The writer of this letter to the Dorking and Leatherhead Advertiser in November 1914 is reminded of Box Hill by scenery near the front. Like many at the time, he writes home to the paper of conditions at the front. Later in the war the reporting of such information was restricted.

population. In November 46 were appointed in Dorking, 8 in Westcott, 22 in Holmwood, 16 in Abinger, 3 in Newdigate, 4 in Capel, 4 in Ockley, 11 in Mickleham and 8 in Wotton.

The civilian population wanted to know what individuals might do to protect their homes should invasion come. In the absence of a national plan, initiatives were taken locally in an ad hoc manner, usually organized and funded by the wealthier and more influential residents of each village. When the High Sheriff suggested the use of rifle club members as guards, Cuthbert Heath offered his rifle range at Anstie Grange to the Holmwood Rifle Club and supplied it with ammunition. In Newdigate Mrs Janson of Newdigate Place initiated and funded a 'Useful Service Brigade' to train men in military skills. It drilled twice a week in the grounds of the school and attended its first church parade, marching to

ENROLMENT OF

SPECIAL CONSTABLES

COUNTY OF SURREY.

THE WAR.

It may be found necessary to enrol a certain number of Special Constables to do duty near their homes in the County of Surrey.

The Chief Constable of Surrey therefore requests that all loyal persons (not under 21 years of age) who may be willing to serve in the capacity of Special Constable, will give their names to the nearest Police Constable of the district in which they reside.

M. L. SANT, Capt.,
Chief Constable of Surrey.

Recruitment poster for Surrey special constables. Such recruitment began immediately on outbreak of the war.

Onward Christian Soldiers with the village Scouts and Fife and Drum band, in late November. It was, adjudged the parish magazine: 'a fine body of men that any town might be proud of.'

In late 1914 Frederick Ernest Green wrote to the *Dorking Advertiser* urging those who could not enlist due to age or infirmity to make themselves efficient 'by drilling and shooting'. He pointed to the small volunteer company in Newdigate. He could not believe, he wrote, that no such volunteer company existed in Dorking 'which has a reputation as a patriotic town with a military tradition' and one that held a strategic position along the line of the North Downs. He also urged the formation of a company to which the men of Beare Green, Capel, Ockley and Holmwood might join as they could reach Dorking easily by bus or rail to join training marches. A Volunteer Training Corps, affiliated with the Central Volunteers Association, was formed in Dorking in November 1914 with some sixty men immediately enrolling. William Dinnage, then a teenager who worked the land with his father, joined

the Dorking Voluntary Training Corps. He later recalled that members were issued with a grey uniform and drilled or trained with guns two or three nights a week, although 14 to 17-year-olds like Dinnage were only admitted as cadets. They were commanded by retired Colonel H.H. Gordon Clark of Mickleham Hall. However, how much the men could do was dictated by the nature of their work: for example, Dinnage and his father, unlike others who had Monday to Saturday jobs, could not go out trench-digging on Sundays.

Such organizations had to be careful to avoid accusations that they might discourage men of military age from enlisting. For men of military age, joining a local defence organization was not to be considered sufficient contribution to the war effort. The Volunteer Training Corps was at pains to stress that anyone under 38 and eligible for Kitchener's Army would not be allowed to join unless they could show a good reason why they had not enlisted. Mrs Janson in Newdigate countered accusations that Newdigate's Useful Service Brigade might be recruiting those who ought to be serving by pointing out that some of the Newdigate youngsters were under 17, others were rejected recruits, some were sole family breadwinners who could not be expected to enlist, and others were over recruitment age. Only a few, she said, 'had no inclination to enlist' but were happy to be of use should circumstances arise.

Lord Kitchener's original call for 100,000 men was not enough. Local papers, local vicars and parish magazines all called for recruits: in the Newdigate parish magazine the Reverend Bird regretted British unpreparedness in not having trained every young man with three years' military service, as the Germans had done, in previous years. The young men of the parish, he insisted: 'should enlist in the Regular Army or join Lord Kitchener's force.' He regretted that all had not done so: 'One could have wished that all the young men in the Parish had regarded it as their duty and privilege to offer themselves in this time of great trouble.' He anticipated, correctly, that the government would be forced to introduce conscription. In early December the Dorking recruitment committee reported a poor turnout at a meeting at the lecture hall in Junction Road. Poor weather had caused an outdoor meeting at the Rotunda to be abandoned but many had stayed away from the indoor meeting as well. It was felt in some quarters that people little understood the war. In early December the Primrose League

arranged a lecture at the Oddfellows Hall, chaired by Holmwood's Colonel Henry H. Helsham Jones, on the causes of the war, with musical accompaniment by the Surrey Yeomanry, in a bid to increase understanding and thereby boost recruitment.

Belgian refugee Albert Vanhove, who found work at Mason's store on the High Street. From the collection of Nicky Vileyn van Hove, Brussels.

By the end of October the town was beginning to come into contact with those who had seen the full effects of war first-hand: refugees and wounded soldiers. Emmeline Pethick-Lawrence of The Mascot in South Holmwood, erstwhile treasurer of Mrs Pankhurst's militant suffragette Women's Social and Political Union, brought a small party

of Belgian refugees to Holmwood. She offered accommodation through the Women's Emergency Corps at The Sundial, a holiday home that she had built for poor London mothers and their children.

Others were housed by the Irish peer, Lord Ashbourne, at his home at Moorhurst in Holmwood. In mid-October, at Reverend Russell Finlay's instigation, the Urban District Council responded to appeals to house some of the thousands of refugees who were arriving in the country. Appeals in the local papers for accommodation saw townspeople offering empty properties, donating furniture and raising money to supply food, fuel and clothing. The Capel Women's Adult Education group met once a week at the school to sew clothes for the Belgians; the Duke of Norfolk allowed them wood from local commons; local coal merchants donated coal; and individuals and households supplied fruit, meat, flowers, poultry and clothing. The first thirty-five refugees arrived at the end of October. By November Grange Cottage and Grove House, both in Horsham Road, 2 Horsham Road, 9 High Street Buildings, 7 Clifton Terrace in Cliftonville, Briar Cottage in Howard Road, Fernfield in Holmwood and Mickleham and Juniper Halls in Mickleham were all hosting Belgian refugees. These included a doctor and an Antwerp factory-owner and their families, and a lieutenant colonel and a commander in the Belgian army. Soon after their arrival, the Maertens, a chemist and his extended family from Ostend and Louvain, and Marie Van Hoeve from Nieuport, who had all found lodgings at 2 Horsham Road, Dorking, could be found visiting the tower on Leith Hill.

In order to help refugees' families in trying to track them down, the *Dorking and Leatherhead Advertiser* published names and addresses of all of those resident in the district. In mid-November the Congregational Church volunteered to find homes for another batch of refugees, including a one-month-old baby who had been named after three kings: George Edward Leopold. Also in mid-November another party was housed at Shrub Hill House, but without access to family wealth or unable to ply their trades, the refugees were reliant on charity. The townspeople undertook regular fund-raising initiatives: concerts at the Oddfellows Hall in the High Street, sales and various appeals. On Wednesday afternoons the Wesleyan Hall on South Street was put at their disposal as a gathering place: calls were made for French books and papers to be donated for use there, and English language classes

were initiated. Dr H. Diendonne of Malines wrote to thank the council and the inhabitants of Dorking for the kindness extended to them. However, the refugees' situation remained precarious. In 1915 the council exempted properties housing refugees from the requirement to pay rates on the grounds that the properties would have been unoccupied but for the Belgians, who were too impoverished to pay.

SATURDAY, OCTOBER 31, 1914.

BELGIAN VISITORS AT DORKING.

The Dorking Committee during the past week have had placed at their disposal by Mr. F. Davey, Grove House, Horsham-road, and by Messrs. Wood and Phillips the living rooms over their premises, No. 9, High-street Buildings, for the reception of Belgian visitors. These have been completely furnished; at Grove House one family is now in residence, and at 9, High-street Buildings, a large family is expected during this week-end. No. 7, Clifton-terrace, Cliftonville, has also been offered to the committee, and is now being furnished for another party of Belgians who are expected early next week. The committee wish through our columns to thank the many residents of Dorking who have kindly provided furniture and rendered much valued assistance in other ways. We understand that it is proposed to hold a social evening for the benefit of our Belgian visitors in the Oddfellows' Hall on Nov. 12th.

In the hope that it may enable them to get in touch with their friends scattered in various parts of the country, we append the names and addresses of Belgian visitors who are now being cared for in this neighbourhood :—

GRANGE COTTAGE, HORSHAM-ROAD, DORKING.

Dr. Henry Dieudonne, 81, Rue Notre Dame, Malines.
Madame Bertha Peeters Dieudonne, wife of the above.
Madame Peeters, widow, 49, Rue Frederick de Merode, Malines.
Madame Rene Michiels, daughter of Dr. Dieudonne, 21, Avenue Jean Stobbaerts, Brussels.
Emilien Michiels, infant son of Madame Michiels.
Therese Torneels, domestic servant, 166, Chaussee de Ternueren, Malines.

GROVE HOUSE, HORSHAM-ROAD, DORKING.

Jules Louis Morisons, 109, Dambruggestreet, Antwerp, factory owner.
Jean Laenens, wife of Emile Peeters, 11, Dambruggestreet, Antwerp.
Francois Laenens, 11, Floris Street, Antwerp, bank agency inspector.
Anna Laenens, 11, Floris Street, Antwerp, sister of Francois Laenens.
Mathilde Jansens, 109, Dambruggestreet, Antwerp.

"BRIAR COTTAGE," HOWARD-ROAD, DORKING.

Madame Jeanne Michiels, 139, Avenue de la Reine, Brussels.
Mlle. Adelard Michiels, same address.
Madame Hilda de Benkelzer, same address.
Mlle. Melanie Michiels, same address.
Madame Clementin Tourgols, 35, Rue due Canal, Louvain.
Mr. Jean Tourgols, her son, same address.
Mr. Edmond Tourgols, her son, same address.
Mlle. Marie Louise Tourgols, her daughter, same address.
Marie Veiminneu, domestic servant, St. Gilles, Termonde, in the service of Madame Michiels.

FERNFIELD, HOLMWOOD.

Fr. Thys-Claes, his wife and four children, of 55, Rue St. Willebrord, Antwerp.
Jos. Van den Broeck-Claes, his wife, three children and the maid-servant, Louise Laureys (of Buggenhout), 137, Antwerpsche Straat, Lierre.
Ferd. Schoop-Smits and his wife, of 46, Rue des Champs, Borgerhout, Antwerp.

JUNIPER HALL, DORKING.

Madame Lucien Dehuy.
M. le Lieutenant-Colonel Dehuy, Commandant 26th Regiment, 2nd Division, convalescent, both from Antwerp (Anvers).

MICKLEHAM HALL.

Madame Omer de Huy and two daughters, Termonde.
Madame Authoon and son, Termonde.

BENCOMB.

Madame Govaerts.
M. le Commandant Joseph Govaerts, 7th Regiment, Antwerp (Anvers).
Mademoiselle Govaerts, Wavre, near Brussels.

The Dorking and Leatherhead Advertiser lists the names of Belgian refugees being housed in the town to assist family members in locating their relatives.

Casualties at the front brought the injured and the convalescent into the district as the British Red Cross set up auxiliary hospitals employing Voluntary Aid Detachment (VAD) nurses across Surrey. The Surrey branch of the Red Cross had been formed in 1907 and its president was the Hon. Mrs Cubitt (wife of Henry Cubitt and later Lady Ashcombe). It eventually administered forty-one hospitals during the war, including Clandon Park and Anstie Grange. By November 1914 several Dorking residents had offered their homes for use as convalescent hospitals: Kirkstall in Dorking; Sondes Place to the west of the town; Leylands (home of the Brooke tea family) in Wotton; Holmwood Lodge (opposite the church in North Holmwood); Cotmandene Lodge; and Arnolds in Beare Green. Wounded Belgian soldiers were the first admissions to the Kirkstall convalescent home in early October.

As the war progressed it was often in the owners' interests to let their mansions as hospitals or to the military. Shortages of staff, as more men left for the army and women took on a wider range of work than domestic service, meant that owners could no longer rely on the scores of low-paid domestic workers, inside and out, needed to run such properties. Also the uncertainties of war hit the investment incomes of many, resulting in necessary economies at home. Anstie Grange saw a reduction in internal staff from twenty-six to three in 1914, with a similar loss in the grounds' staff. When the military left Deepdene in mid-1915, there were ten groundsmen caring for it; by 1917 that had been reduced to one caretaker. Dorking's grandest mansion never returned to residential use. The decline that saw many of Dorking's mansions falling into disrepair was often never reversed: many were demolished or their lands broken up and auctioned as plots in the years between the two world wars.

From early September newly-recruited territorials were also expected in town. The council was keen to encourage the military authorities to billet troops locally, in the hope that the arrival of men with money to spend would be good for struggling businesses. When, after several disappointments, the Yeomanry finally arrived in late October, two companies were billeted at the Public Halls and one at Deepdene. The remainder were accommodated in private houses. The Yeomanry's horses were stabled at Denbies, at Chalk Pits House and Home Farm, and at the White Horse Hotel in the High Street. Training

A member of the Surrey Yeomanry on horseback at Deepdene. The Surrey Yeomanry were encamped at Deepdene from late 1914 to mid-1915.

took place at Ranmore and the Bury Hill estate. The presence of troops saw a steady stream of accidents, such as a runaway artillery gun on Box Hill and several motorcycle collisions. Most seriously, Private William Golding, a groom from London serving with the Yeomanry, died of a head wound at the cottage hospital in mid-October after falling from his horse in the stable yard at Bury Hill. The horse that threw him was one of five that had been loaned to the Yeomanry by Henry Cubitt (before the war they had been ridden by his sons, now serving in France).

The Yeomanry troops were popular in town; the trustees of the Wesleyan Hall in South Street raised funds to convert the hall for their recreational use and every week townspeople organized musical performances for them there. The favour was repaid in December when the Yeomanry gave a concert for the people of Dorking.

The community applied itself to supporting those who had left. The papers were full of appeals for 'comforts' that the army was unable to provide and local women organized initiatives to supply them. Most of these initiatives were started by committed individuals acting on reports of hardship. When it was discovered that the authorities could not supply blankets to all recruits and men were walking all night to keep warm, an appeal went out to supply blankets. E.L. Chaldecott collected and supplied jumpers to the Gurkhas. Miss Chichester, daughter of Canon Chichester at St Martin's, collected and sent off parcels to local men. The ladies of Newdigate's needlework class worked eight hours a day making articles to send to the troops. In South Holmwood schoolchildren knitted with materials supplied by Mrs Habershon of Brook Lodge. The girls of St Paul's School knitted scarves and socks and sent them to Portsmouth, while the girls and teachers of the Dorking British School undertook needlework and knitting for soldiers, sailors and the Red Cross. By December they had made 57 garments from donated material, and 190 from material supplied from a fund to which teachers subscribed every month. In late 1914 Mrs Winfield, who ran a smallholding at Cudworth near Newdigate, began collecting bandages, pillow slips and linen to be sent to Calais every month, after a doctor friend wrote telling her that wounded men were arriving in hospitals with newspapers wrapping their wounds. Other Newdigate villagers collected books for British prisoners of war in Germany and left them at the village Post Office from where they were collected for shipping. Mrs Bell of Moor Lodge in Holmwood organized parcels for the prisoners. When the *Dorking Advertiser* promoted a campaign to supply cigarettes and tobacco to the troops, Hilda Walker of Wathen Road collected individual cigarettes on the streets of Dorking and supplied 510 of them to the editor. By December 4,641 packets had been supplied.

Community initiatives also fund-raised for those at home. Concerts, plays and fancy dress events were a constant in the monthly social calendar to raise money for the Dorking Red Cross and for the patients at the hospital at Kirkstall, for the Belgian refugees and for the Prince of Wales' Relief Fund. In December an auction to raise funds for the Belgians was held at The Wheatsheaf. Children from Dene Street paraded the streets in fancy dress representing the allied nations collecting in pennies; others performed a playlet dressed as fairies. At

Christmas, funds were raised for a concert and tea at St Paul's for the Belgians, and for a 'Treat' for their children and for the children of those who were serving overseas as the town came together to support those who were suffering.

As the first Christmas of the war approached, there was little in the local papers that did not in some way relate to the conflict, whether reports of casualties or of fund-raising for troops, hospitals or refugees. Photographs of the dead appeared next to adverts for turkeys and geese. Even the traders' adverts brought the war to mind, tempting shoppers with ideal present selections – warm clothes, tobacco and chocolate – for sons, husbands and brothers overseas. Although the mood remained generally positive about the morality and conduct of the war, time, money and resources were short and, with loved ones away and in danger, individuals were in need of support. In Holmwood weekly evening gatherings were organized with a programme of 'straight speakers' at the village hall to take people's minds off the

An advert for R.J. Cook's in the High Street in December of 1914 comments that foodstuffs are selling at higher than usual prices.

war. Women were invited to bring their sewing and men their pipes to gatherings in Mickleham. However, it was churches that took the leading role in supporting the community. In Newdigate a Day of Intercession was held for 'more things are wrought by prayer than this

Clarks & Co. of Dorking advertise suitable Christmas presents for family members serving with the forces, Christmas 1914.

Don't Forget Your

Soldier and Sailor Friends.

CHEESMAN & BROMLEY

are well provided with warm Shirts,

Vests, Socks, Mufflers, Balaclava Caps,

Cap Comforters and Woollen Belts,

Handkerchiefs, Gloves, Mittens, etc.,

at Economical Prices, in many cases

lower than London Store Prices.

Cheesman and Bromley encourage families to think of loved ones in the forces in order to promote Christmas buying.

world dreams of and we cannot expect to win unless we are earnest in our supplications before the Throne of God,' claimed Reverend Bird. Perhaps not everyone was convinced, as attendance was only fair: 'I wish I could have said there was not a man or woman in Newdigate who did not attend one of the services that day,' commented the vicar in the next parish magazine, as he urged villagers to pray for victory every day.

Missing in Action: Henry Harman Young

Second Lieutenant Henry Harman Young (1893–1915) was one of those who left immediately upon war being declared. The son of Major Henry Harman Young, a retired spirit merchant who was second-in-command of the Dorking reserve company, Henry grew up at Balgowan, a large house in Harrow Road, Dorking with his brothers, Kenneth and John, and his sisters, Barbara and Bessie. All three brothers served during the war. After leaving Charterhouse School he was articled to a firm of auctioneers and surveyors in Dorking.

Second Lieutenant Henry Harman Young (1893–1915).

Henry went out to France with the Artists Rifles in October 1914. He was promoted to sergeant in December and became an instructor at the machine-gun school in St Omer. In May 1915 he became a second lieutenant in the 3rd Battalion, Royal Fusiliers. He went missing during the Second Battle of Ypres shortly afterwards. His family appealed to the King of Spain to intercede with the Germans for news of their son. In December the Spanish Ambassador to Berlin reported that Henry was in a prisoner of war camp. In fact, he had died on 24 May, aged 21.

In 1921 Major Harman Young received a letter from a German woman in Stuttgart whose son had found Henry severely injured on the battlefield and had given water to the dying young man. The German soldier had lived in England and was able to speak to Henry, and asked his own mother to relay the message to his parents (which she did many years later) that their son had been taken care of before he died. The German soldier was subsequently also killed.

A Military Family at War: the Heaths of Anstie Grange

Cuthbert Heath OBE (1859–1939) was born into a military family. His father, Admiral Sir Leopold Heath (1817–1907), had built Anstie Grange, between Holmwood and Coldharbour, in the 1860s. Three of Sir Leopold's five sons followed him into the military. Cuthbert's brother, Major General Sir Gerard Moore Heath (1863–1929), was chief engineer to the 1st Army in France under Sir Douglas Haig; another brother, Admiral Sir Herbert Heath (1861–1954), became Second Sea Lord. Cuthbert, however, suffered from deafness, precluding a military career.

Cuthbert Heath dressed for hunting. (Photo reproduced courtesy of J.J. Heath-Caldwell)

Considered the dullard of the family, he was set up in a Lloyd's insurance syndicate. With unexpected aptitude, he made a fortune. He also transformed Lloyd's of London from a marine insurer to the general insurer of international renown that it is today. He was known for

Major General Sir Gerard Moore Heath, chief engineer to the 1st Army under Haig, was one of Cuthbert Heath's brothers. So high-ranking were Cuthbert's siblings that attempts were made to infiltrate the Anstie household. Cuthbert's daughter Genesta recalled in her autobiography that in 1915 a woman purporting to be Danish applied for a job as her governess and was discovered to have been a German spy. (Photo reproduced courtesy of J.J. Heath-Caldwell)

Admiral Sir Herbert Heath, Second Sea Lord during the First World War, was also Cuthbert Heath's brother. He had grown up at Anstie Grange. He was the senior admiral of the cruiser line at the Battle of Jutland in May 1916, and was subsequently given command of the Channel Fleet. He was appointed Second Sea Lord and Chief of Naval Personnel in 1917. (Photo reproduced courtesy of J.J. Heath-Caldwell)

his innovations, including issuing the first motor insurance and burglary policies. At the outbreak of war he was living with his wife Caroline, nee Gambier, at Anstie Grange, a twenty-six-bedroom mansion that was host to shooting parties, hunts and balls.

Cuthbert Heath immediately set to recruiting, speaking at recruitment meetings, giving pep talks at Anstie to local men who volunteered and setting up a recruitment office at Lloyd's of London where volunteers could be sworn in. In 1914 he allowed the local rifle club to use his rifle range and supplied them with ammunition. In 1915 he invited the London Civil Service Rifles to drill in his grounds. Perhaps unsurprisingly, given the family's military record,

his son and his seven nephews were in uniform before the end of 1914.

The effects of the war were immediately felt at Anstie where an indoor staff of twenty-six, plus chauffeurs, stablemen and gardeners outside, dwindled as employees either volunteered for the military (or were later conscripted), or moved into war-related work. Heath's daughter, Genesta, who was 15 when the war broke out, recalled the indoor staff reducing to three. Despite his commitment to recruiting, on occasion he applied to the Dorking Military Tribunal for exemptions from service for key members of his staff, most notably his gamekeeper.

Heath and his family threw themselves into work for the war effort. Cuthbert was asked by the government to draw up an insurance scheme to cover the public against losses from action by hostile aircraft. Throughout the war he bankrolled the struggling Surrey Union Hunt, regularly writing cheques for £500 to keep the hunt going, despite shortages of horses and the conscription of hunt staff. (The government encouraged hunting throughout the war in order to ensure that horse stocks were maintained.)

Cuthbert's brother, Arthur Raymond Heath, who lived nearby at North Breache Manor near Ewhurst and then at Kitlands, involved himself with the Surrey Guides, the Soldiers and Sailors Help Society, the Dorking War Pensions Committee and the special constables.

Arthur Raymond Heath. Cuthbert's brother, the former MP for Louth, came to live at Kitlands, one of the adjacent family estates, in 1915. He and his wife Flora were barred from Anstie after a falling-out between Flora and his sister-in-law, Caroline. Arthur Raymond and Flora's son, Raymond Leopold Grieg Heath, was badly wounded in the fight for the Menin Road at Ypres in October 1914 but recovered and was subsequently killed by a sniper on 25 September 1915 at the Battle of Loos, aged 30. A memorial service was held in October 1915 at which a member of his company played The Last Post. A stained-glass window at Christ Church, Coldharbour, commemorates his life, depicting troops in battledress. (Photo reproduced courtesy of J.J. Heath-Caldwell)

Arthur Raymond's wife, Flora, trained in massage and worked at the Leatherhead Red Cross hospital, later providing convalescence to shell-shocked soldiers at Kitlands. Arthur and Flora lost their son, Raymond Leopold Grieg Heath, at the Battle of Loos in 1915. His life is commemorated in a striking window at Coldharbour church.

Heath's most significant contribution to the war effort was in offering up his mansion as a hospital in 1916, for which he was awarded an OBE. After the war Anstie returned to family use. During the Second World War it was again occupied by the military, housing the headquarters of Queen Alexandra's Royal Military Nurses into the 1950s. The family never returned and Anstie Grange is now split into apartments.

Captain Raymond Leopold Grieg Heath. (Photo courtesy of Ewhurst Fallen)

The memorial window to Raymond Leopold Grieg Heath of the Queen's (Royal West Surrey) Regiment at Christ Church, Coldharbour, depicting First World War troops in battledress worshipping on the battlefield. The church also displays the Union flag flown over Anstie Grange when it was a military hospital from 1916–18.

CHAPTER 3

1915: Invasions

Our Dorking was a dull old town
Until the soldiers came our way,
But now the streets are bright and gay
Because of all the lads in brown.
For when they swagger up and down
All very eager for the fray
And they, we hope, will win renown
Upon the all important day.
Trade was dull, and often nil
Before the soldiers made it bright
And shopmen have a bulging till
From early morning till late at night.
And many a pretty Dorking maid
Has lost her heart I am afraid.

Written by a local schoolboy, this poem appeared in the *Dorking and Leatherhead Advertiser* in 1915, summing up the changes to Dorking as it became a garrison town. All over Britain, recalled reservists, territorials and volunteers with Kitchener's 'New Army' were being trained and formed into units before being sent to relieve and support the regular army in France. Troops were billeted on local populations for the first time in a hundred years and between late 1914 and mid-1915 several thousand troops were billeted in empty buildings in Dorking as they trained on the surrounding hills. The Surrey Yeomanry were traditionally based in the west and north of Surrey, and had often

The Public Halls on West Street became the headquarters of the Surrey Yeomanry stationed in Dorking in 1915.

held training camps at Denbies before the war. In late 1914 several hundred men were billeted in Dorking and by 1915 Yeomanry troops were occupying the Public Halls, which also housed the fire brigade, on West Street, parts of Deepdene and the new Betchworth Golf Club clubhouse. Some of the company were encamped at Sondes Place.

January 1915 saw between 3,000 and 4,000 more troops arriving in Dorking as the 179th Brigade of the 60th (2/2nd London) Division of territorials formed up in the Dorking and Leatherhead area. The 2/14th Battalion London Regiment (London Scottish), the 2/15th Battalion London Regiment (Civil Service Rifles) and the 2/16th Battalion London Regiment (Queen's Westminster Rifles) were all billeted in the town. Other brigades were billeted in Reigate, Redhill and Leatherhead. The division also comprised companies of the Royal Army Medical Corps (RAMC), who trained in the town, and the Royal Field Artillery (RFA) that camped at Milton Heath. The composer Ralph Vaughan Williams, who had grown up at Leith Hill Place, found himself posted to the town of his youth with the RAMC with which he was serving as an orderly. Empty shops and houses in the town and

Members of the Surrey Yeomanry medical team larking about for the cameras at the Deepdene camp. The photograph is captioned 'Surrey Yeomanry Butchers'.

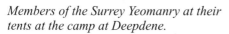

Members of the Surrey Yeomanry at their tents at the camp at Deepdene.

Portraits of members of the Surrey Yeomanry taken while at the Deepdene camp.

surrounding villages were requisitioned to accommodate the troops and householders were called upon to house those who could not be accommodated in empty buildings.

In February 1915 an anonymous London Scots soldier named 'Wullie' wrote in the *London Scottish Regimental Gazette* of his impressions of Dorking, and in particular of its public houses and their caves: 'It has gotten twa railway stations, a wheen Kirks, and an awful lot of public hooses, ane wi a great muckel cave awa doon doon under the foundations' (a reference to the caves lying beneath many Dorking shops and inns). Some, he reported, were lucky with their billets and found themselves in fine parlours with kind-hearted landladies; others

28. Civil Service Mess Wesley Hall   F.W.Tigwell Dorking.

Members of the Prince of Wales' Own Civil Service Rifles at Wesleyan Hall in South Street, Dorking, 1915. Wesleyan Hall was adapted to provide a place of recreation for troops stationed at Dorking.

The London Scottish Regiment at Deepdene Vale, 1915.

London Scottish Band.

F. W. Tigwell,
Dorking.
Photo. C.P.P. No 16.

The London Scottish Regiment Band photographed at Dorking, 1915.

'F' Company, The London Scottish Regiment, photographed in Dorking, 1915.

The London Scottish Regiment in training in Ansell Road, Dorking.

London Scottish Training in Dorking

The London Scottish Regiment kit inspection in Rothes Road, Dorking.

The London Scottish on parade at Wathen Road, Dorking.

The London Scottish on the march near Dorking, 1915.

The London Scottish returning from church parade at St Martin's.

slept on the floor of an empty sweet shop. Rations were doled out initially on the street corner, where dogs congregated in hope, and someone in town presented the commanding officer with a goat that the troops tried to lead out in front of the bagpipes as a mascot.

Shortly after arrival chickenpox broke out among the troops, as humorously related in the *Gazette*: 'Dear Jock – Ye ta'k aboot fowls? You should jist see the Dorking chickens! The Congregational Ha' is fu' o' them, graand birds! Well guarded in the red-brick buildings, and o them has been sent awa' tae the hospital.' 'A' Company was quarantined in the Congregational Hall. There they upset the minister in the church next door with their piping during services. However, the people of Dorking were generally fond of the bagpipes. The correspondent writes of six or seven pipers resident and playing in the town: 'no' bad for Dorking eh? There's ane o' them that is daein' roarin' weel doon at the Star and Garter, whaur he blaws his head aff every nicht to make the CO enjoy his denner!' 'Wullie' records that local women showered the pipers with gifts of 'bawbees', knitted 'gravats' and packets of 'Scottish Abdullahs', so taken were they with the piping.

While billeted in Dorking the troops undertook battalion training and drill at Denbies, went on route marches up Box Hill and to Headley and Leith Hill, and carried out tactical training exercises at Leigh. They attended lectures in the town centre, and were sent by special train to Sandwich for musketry training. The RAMC practised stretcher drill on the slopes of Box Hill and Ranmore, and on the town streets, and took route marches to Guildford and back. On 22 January the London

Scottish marched from Dorking to Epsom Downs, where, with other troops stationed in the area, they were inspected by Lord Kitchener: 20,000 men paraded in 8 inches of snow for several hours, resulting in the death of one of the Dorking contingent from pneumonia a few days later.

The town welcomed the troops and seems to have been a pleasant posting. A branch of the Young Men's Christian Association was established at the Oddfellows' Hall, providing a place for troops to socialize, read and play games. The men paraded to church, and on occasion Ralph Vaughan Williams led a choir of fellow military volunteers at St Martin's. Local ladies challenged the sergeants of the

The Royal Army Medical Corps in training in Myrtle Road, Dorking, 1915. The composer Ralph Vaughan Williams was serving with the RAMC and stationed in Dorking. (Photos reproduced with permission of Eric Mansfield and Susannah Horne)

The Royal Army Medical Corps on parade in Myrtle Road, Dorking, outside Warne & Co. Automobile Engineers, 1915.

London Scottish to a shooting match at the rifle range, Cuthbert Heath invited the Civil Service Rifles to train at his rifle range at Anstie Grange, and locals had to be urged to desist from buying drinks for men in training for the front. The 'test' faced by the men required more than the usual fitness for football or cricket, stressed local vicars, so the offer of a beer was not appropriate. The populace was urged to give extra socks, scarves, tobacco or chocolate to demonstrate their appreciation instead.

In order to prevent drunkenness among the troops, licensing restrictions were imposed in January 1915. Licensed victuallers were prohibited from selling alcohol after 9 in the evening and before 9 in the morning. While appreciated in the town, the move was met with dismay in the villages and among suppliers of alcohol. A petition of forty licensees demanded that the restrictions only apply in Dorking Urban District and Rural District areas, and not in

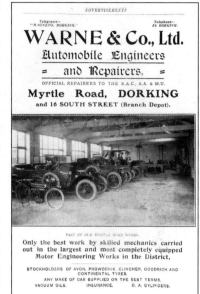

Advert for Warne's Automobile repairers from the Holmesdale Directory of 1914. Photographs show troops parading outside Warne's premises in Myrtle Road.

the further-flung parishes where there were no troops billeted. Almost immediately William James, licensee of the Queen's Head at the corner of South Street and Horsham Road, was fined for selling beer in prohibited hours to Mr Bond, the Holmwood baker (James's wife had drawn beer for Mr Bond after 9pm). Soon afterwards Frank Pratt of the Station Hotel was summoned for serving 'prohibited intoxicants' to members of the Army Service Corps (twelve of whom were billeted at the hotel), who were attending a concert after 9pm.

The influx of several thousand men put a strain on local services, particularly on sanitary arrangements. In January 1915 the council sanitary inspector served notices on the owners of premises where troops were billeted, requiring them to provide latrines as a matter of urgency. Letters to the paper complained that not only were latrines not being provided at billets and encampments, but there were no public conveniences in the town either. The problem was not quickly

solved; in August the council was still having to remove excreta from the military camp at Sondes Place, at a cost of 21 shillings a week.

The small town baths, which were operated by the council in Station Road, also had to accommodate hugely increased numbers. In May 1915 the council arranged for the provision of soap and towels for the Argyll and Sutherland Highlanders on Wednesday evenings and Sunday mornings, and for two workmen to clean and clear the baths, at a cost to the regiment of £1 weekly. Similar arrangements were made for the Royal Field Artillery and the Surrey Yeomanry.

Cleanliness and waste problems resulted as much from the increased number of horses in the area as from the troops. Wherever the troops went, stabling had to be found for the large numbers of horses that pulled heavy equipment, field guns and supplies. The Surrey Yeomanry's horses were stabled at the chalk pits and fields below Denbies (now the Municipal Recycling Centre), and at Sondes Place Farm. The Royal Field Artillery kept their horses in Westcott, in a field and on the common. The movement of these animals, particularly when pulling heavy guns, caused serious damage to the footpaths and roads, and the council faced large repair bills to keep the roads usable.

However, transport was crucial to the war effort. Most military and civilian business was conducted by horse-drawn transport or by rail. Moving large numbers of troops around a rural area was a logistical problem requiring additional infrastructure. A railway halt had to be built for the Westcott Rifle Range at Denbies to enable troops to travel

The Royal Field Artillery encamped on Milton Heath at the foot of Ranmore in 1915. Note the large number of horses and a plane as well as the tents.

Hand-drawn cartoons published in the London Scottish Regimental Gazette in March 1915. One humorously compares a march back from Epsom to Dorking on 22 January 1915 (in the snow) with Napoleon's 1812 retreat from Moscow. The other shows a stylish young woman being ogled by four men dressed in different military uniforms: testament to the variety of troops then stationed in the town.

there to use it. In 1916, when military rifle ranges were built on the north side of the railway line at nearby Coomb Farm, the South Eastern Railway Company opened two wooden platforms as a temporary station for soldiers using the range. The so-called 'Westcott Range Halt' was not open for public use.

The troops in training had no idea where they would eventually be posted and throughout 1915 the town was awash with rumour. An anonymous Scotsman sent up the atmosphere in the *Gazette*, reporting talk that the quartermaster had received 1,000 pith helmets, meaning that the battalion was to be posted to Honolulu or Hong Kong, and that a company was to be sent to join Shackleton in the Antarctic to prevent the German fleet from reaching the South Pole.[1]

There were also rumours of spies in the area. One night, members of the London Scottish noticed red, green and yellow lights flashing on a hillside which they considered suspicious. They called for assistance from some navy men and crawled up the hillside, only to find that their signals were railway lamps and that the flashing was caused by trees blowing in front of them in the wind. It is difficult to surmise who the supposed spies might have been trying to communicate with, but that the incident was investigated suggests that

1 The polar explorer, Ernest Shackleton (1874–1922), had been due to sail on an attempt to cross the continent of Antarctica on the eve of war. On offering the services of his crew to the war effort, he was ordered to proceed on his mission.

the possibility of spies operating in the neighbourhood was not considered unlikely.

The 179th Brigade left Dorking by special train at the end of March 1915, and the Surrey Yeomanry in June. The 13th (Reserve) Division of the Argyll and Sutherland Highlanders, who had arrived in April, also left in June. The council commended the troops' behaviour and lack of drunkenness and approached billeting officers in Reigate, asking them to send more troops to Dorking, for troops brought in money and tradesmen were happy to have their business.

By mid-1915 the effects of many men being away in the military was having an impact on the community. When conscription was brought in agricultural workers would be considered vital to the economy, but voluntary enlistment in the early days of the war had seen many of the area's skilled farm workers enlisting or being recalled as reservists or territorials. In June 1915, with the first harvest since mobilization imminent, Surrey County Council questioned whether there were sufficient labourers to bring in the harvest. It began compiling a list of men who could assist in an emergency. When asked to supply a list of men in the Dorking area who would be available in case of emergency to gather in the harvest, the Urban District Council responded that there were no men available. It also began to encourage the keeping of pigs and poultry to boost local food supplies, relaxing regulations to enable more people to do so.

All organizations were affected by the decline in manpower. Church parades were thinner with the absence of the territorials. Parish magazines called out for tenors and lost choirmasters. Female bell-

---

Official Rumours at Dorking.

THAT the Quartermaster has received a thousand pith helmets to be distributed to the Battalion prior to its departure for Honolulu or Hong Kong. The camels have already been inoculated.

Owing to the shortage of fig rations, the Battalion has been ordered to Smyrna. Figs will be worn with a regimental ribbon, which will be tied in a bow at the back. Army Form B. F. 144.

That a double Company is to be sent to join Shackleton in the Antarctic and so prevent the German fleet from reaching the South Pole. The Quarter-Master of each Company will be responsible for the issue of snow shoes to each platoon. Army Order K.B.A. 256.

That the regimental mascot is to be sent to Chelsea for a course of training in the Machine Gun Section.

That the regimental barber is to be court martialled for being absent three days without leave.

ALEC. GOW AND THE PARSON.

Gow says to a Dorking parson, who is visiting a sick billet. " I would gie they chaps a glass o' whisky. In my pairt of Scotland where I come frae there are no doctors and we gie the folk that are no weel a drap o' the cratur. " And if that does them no good," asks the parson, " what do you do ?" " Gie them anither drop," says Gow. Just then the regimental M.O. appears, and after looking at the patients orders them castor oil and no duty. After the doctor retires the parson asks if that was a Scotch doctor. " Yes," says Gow. " he is." " Well, why did *he* not order whisky ? " " Na, na he's a canny man, is oor doctor, he orders castor oil and he taks the dram tae himsel'."

THE ladies of Dorking have challenged the Sergeants of the Second Battalion to a shooting match at their range. but owing to the movements of the troops this has had to be postponed.
There is great competition for inclusion in the team, and many duels are impending.

Alec. Gow and the Parson. An amusing story reported in the London Scottish Regimental Gazette, March 1915.

The Army Service Corps, officers and NCOs, at Dorking in 1915.

The Army Service Corps on parade in Dorking, 1915.

Troops leaving Dorking via Westcott Road towards Guildford on 28 February 1915.

ringers took over at St Martin's. Newdigate Choral Society gave up preparations for the annual Leith Hill Musical Competitions before the end of 1914 due to a lack of tenors and basses. By the end of the year the Musical Competitions, established in 1905 and participated in by choirs from all the villages surrounding Dorking and Leith Hill, had announced that competitions would be suspended for the duration of the war. The Beare Green Prosecuting Society's annual dinner, held for over 100 years, was cancelled in 1915, never to be re-established. The Dorking British School announced that it would not celebrate its centenary in 1916 with so many of its ex-pupils away on military service.

Those organizations that suffered the most were those reliant on men of military age. Voluntary fire brigades were particularly affected, not always because men had joined up but because their time and energies had been diverted to other duties. At the outbreak of war thirteen of Holmwood's voluntary fire brigade signed up as special constables, rendering them unavailable for fire duty. By January 1915

By 1915 ringing the bells at St Martin's in Dorking had been taken over by an all-female team. With many men away on active service and others serving as special constables or replacing volunteer firemen, there were fewer men available with the time to carry out their usual community activities.

temporary probationary firemen had been appointed in their place. Mickleham village had found itself in difficulties even earlier, with Boy Scouts taking up some of the work of the volunteer brigade as early as September 1914.

Although there were not general food shortages, the increased demand for coal for military transport and war supplies resulted in price increases and shortages and the council had to intervene to ensure supplies to local customers. In September 1915 it approached local coal merchants to attempt to fix a price for the purchase of small quantities of coal by individuals in the coming winter. In the outlying parishes coal clubs (to which poorer households subscribed all year to receive their winter coal) found that they had insufficient funds to supply their subscribers and were forced to turn to charities to make up the difference between what had been paid in and the increased price of coal.

Mrs W.J. Rose on her Post Office delivery round during the war when a large percentage of local postmen were in the military.

Despite their own difficulties, the civilian population was anxious to support the troops at the front. In November Margaret Longman (of the publishing family) and Evangeline, Lady Farrer, of Abinger Hall, established Dorking's Hospital Supply Depot at Nower Lodge. Owned by Captain Barclay of Bury Hill, the Lodge was converted into work rooms to make supplies for hospitals. The scheme was funded by fêtes, sales, concerts and fund-raisers, and (from March 1917) by donation from the fund-raising Dorking Waste Paper Depot, which collected waste paper for recycling in order to raise money for work of national importance. Some subscribed to raise funds, some walked in to donate their time, giving their bus fares to the scheme, while others gave furniture or loaned sewing machines, tools and benches, or supplied wood for packing cases. Some offered free advertising; other businesses sharpened knives and scissors free of charge. Working parties

were established in Abinger, Betchworth, Newdigate, Ockley, Ranmore, at The Redlands in Holmwood and The Rookery in Westcott, while others knitted at home. Laundries at the great houses of Wigmore (at Beare Green), Abinger Hall and Denbies washed garments, cloths and towels. The depot supplied war hospitals at home and overseas, casualty clearing stations and ambulances. Paying tribute to the volunteers in 1919 when the depot closed, the *Dorking and Leatherhead Advertiser* reported that the volunteers had worked through heat and snow, through anxiety and personal sorrow, and had never failed to 'toil and not to seek for rest'. The hope of mitigating some of the sufferings of the sick and wounded was the cord that drew them, reported the editorial, 'a cord which could never break'.

Evangeline ('Eva'), Lady Farrer of Abinger, was a founder of the Leith Hill Musical Competitions. When the competitions were abandoned for the duration of the war she was instrumental in establishing the Dorking War Supply Depot. (Portrait by Charles Geoffroy-Dechaume)

All over the villages volunteers were working on their own initiatives. In Newdigate a group made sandbags from home or in group meetings, cutting out the material and sewing it ready for use, to be collected and taken to Holmwood Station. By mid-1915 the small team had made 1,700 sandbags for the defence of British troops. In the same village Miss Seward Hill of Fairholme collected for the Bovril fund run by Kate Dickens (daughter of the novelist) to supply hot Bovril to the troops. Letters were regularly published in parish magazines from grateful recipients of medical supplies: when Newdigate's Estelle Winfield sent two boxes of bandages, shirts and linen to the Sophie Berthelot Hospital in Calais, a doctor there wrote to say that those at home little understood the scenes overseas. When a local soldier wrote home to say that he had only had two cigarettes in five days, the editor of the *Dorking and Leatherhead Advertiser* set up a fund to send tobacco to the battlefields.

By January 1915 one million volunteers had been enlisted in the British army. However, casualties at the front were high, estimated by the end of May 1915 at 50,000 killed with 50,000 missing. The town alone lost 5 men at the Second Battle of Ypres between April and May

Certificate issued to schoolboy Eric Phillips of Dorking from the Overseas Club in acknowledgement of his having contributed to Christmas gifts provided by the club to soldiers of the Empire. Children in Dorking contributed by knitting for the soldiers and raising money for cigarettes.

1915, 15 at Arras and Vimy Ridge in May, and would lose 12 more between April and December during the abortive Gallipoli campaign (which cost something in the region of 50,000 allied lives). By September another 6 had been lost at Loos, 15 at the Third Battle of Ypres between August and October, and a further 4 at Cambrai.

Even before these setbacks, voluntary enlistment had fallen back. In February the *Surrey Advertiser* noted that the numbers coming forward were not as high as they had been, and many of those coming forward were found to be unfit for service. With positions in France and Belgium entrenched and immobile, Kitchener was now planning on a war lasting three years but the levels of voluntary recruitment being achieved in early 1915 would not be sufficient for a prolonged war.

The government still hoped to avoid conscription and made strenuous efforts to encourage men to enlist voluntarily. Every Tuesday night in Guildford those who had enlisted from the surrounding areas,

Local men had their photographs taken in uniform before leaving for the front. Ken Harris (top right) of Spring Cottages, Westcott, was a keen member of Dorking Cycling Club. Frank Hardy (bottom left) and William Shearburn (top left) both lived in Dorking. Shearburn was a member of the building family that had constructed much of the town in the decades preceding the war. All three survived the conflict.

A wartime wedding at South Holmwood. On 15 May 1915 Helen (Nellie) Spencer of Stockrydons at Beare Green married Herbert Mason, a private in the Queen's 9th Lancers. Before enlisting, Mason had been a groom at the stables of Colonel Henry H. Helsham-Jones at Redlands in Holmwood. There was an increase in marriages in the early years of the war as couples hurried to marry before enlistment or conscription. (Photo reproduced with permission of Jayne Simms)

including Dorking, marched through the town and the *Surrey Advertiser* recorded the number from Dorking and Reigate, Leatherhead, Godalming and Farnham who had joined up. Parishes and schools published lists of those serving, as well as those who died, as encouragement (and shame) to those remaining. Parishes also compared their records: 'Our list is quite a good one,' commented Reverend Bird of Newdigate in June 1915, reporting sixty-two men serving and three killed, 'though there are parishes with a smaller population which beat us.'

In May the Queen's (Royal West Surrey) Regiment held a recruiting march from Reigate via Leigh and Holmwood to Dorking. The marchers met the Dorking recruiting committee at the Rotunda after parading the streets with a bugle band and the pipes of the Argyll and Sutherland Highlanders. Crowds gathered to watch the inspection by Henry Cubitt. Addressing the crowd, Mr Pardon-Howe, leader of the Urban District Council, said that Dorking needed to do its bit towards the 300,000 men needed by Lord Kitchener and urged that the town should not be bettered by Reigate. Cubitt encouraged local men to join the Queen's now, rather than waiting, thus ensuring that they would serve with their own 'pals' from their own town. They would be celebrated at home: on Empire Day, he reminded them, the names of 200 ex-pupils of St Martin's School now serving had been read out.

Registration was an attempt to boost voluntary enlistment and to avoid having to resort to conscription. Brought in by the National Registration Act 1915, it allowed for the creation of a register of all persons, male and female, between the ages of 15 and 65 who were not members of the armed services. Registration would provide the manpower statistics needed to reveal the number of men still available and not enlisted. Armed with accurate figures, government and the military would be able to determine which groups should be targeted for recruitment (by advertising, door-to-door calls asking them to attest for service if required and, in some cases, by shaming), and which should be retained in civil employment. Men who were identified as being engaged in vital occupations were known as 'starred' as their names were marked with a black star on official records. They wore 'On War Service' badges and were issued with certificates declaring that they were engaged on war work. These badges protected the wearers from comment and criticism.

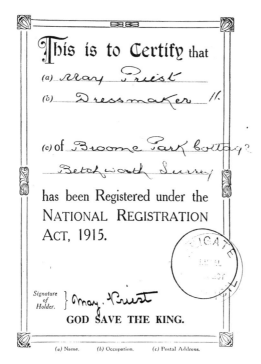

This is to Certify that

(a) *Mary Priest*

(b) *Dressmaker* //.

(c) of *Broome Park cottage?*
Betchworth Surrey

has been Registered under the
NATIONAL REGISTRATION
ACT, 1915.

Signature of Holder. } *May. Priest*

GOD SAVE THE KING.

(a) Name.   (b) Occupation.   (c) Postal Address.

National Registration Card of Mary Priest, a dressmaker living at Broome Park Cottages in Brockham. Registration was brought in by the National Registration Act 1915. It allowed for the creation of a register of all persons, male and female, between the ages of 15 and 65 who were not members of the services. It was a precursor to conscription in creating manpower statistics that revealed the number of men still available and not enlisted. This enabled the authorities to determine which groups should be targeted for recruitment (and later conscription) and which should be retained in civil employment.

By mid-1915 there were still at least two million men of military age in the country who had not volunteered for service. Lord Derby was appointed director of recruitment and the king appealed for men of all classes to come forward. From local pulpits vicars assured the population that the souls of the dead were at peace. Local rallies followed, with a particularly large one at Redhill. However, the local paper was full of casualty lists – of the dead, wounded and missing – and men came home on leave with tales of horror, making recruitment increasingly difficult.

In order to bring forward the 35,000 men a week needed in France and Belgium to replace those killed and wounded and to rotate those in service, Lord Derby instituted a scheme whereby men could indicate their willingness to serve when needed by giving a voluntary undertaking to join up later when called on to do so. (The idea was that the government would know that the men were available, and the men would know that they would only be required when men of the same marital status and age were called up.) Some saw the so-called 'Derby

scheme' as a step towards inevitable conscription; others hoped that its effectiveness would mean that conscription would not be needed. Nevertheless, more than half the men available for military service still failed to attest.

In Dorking the council set up a committee of three to establish a local register in July 1915. For obvious reasons the local registrar of births, marriages and deaths was co-opted onto the committee. A recruitment tribunal was set up to consider personal circumstances in November 1915. The tribunal rented premises in South Street, its role being as much to prevent civilians with vital skills and experience from enlisting as to encourage as many as possible into uniform. Mr Clegg, the council surveyor, made several attempts to join the army, offering to go if the council would make his army pay up to what he then earned in civilian life. Instead, the council applied for a badge of exemption in order to keep him in Dorking.

Threats of financial hardship, particularly to families left behind in an era when women's employment options were few and wages low, prevented many from volunteering. In a letter to the *Dorking and Leatherhead Advertiser* in late 1914, smallholder and writer on agricultural labour issues Frederick Ernest Green of Baringsfield in Cudworth near Newdigate commented that although strong young married men ought to enlist, 'one can hardly blame them for not doing so whilst the miserable pittance allowed to a soldier's childless widow remains at 7s 6d.'

The obituary of teacher Edmund Vialls, printed in the *Dorking High School Magazine* on his death in the summer term of 1918, highlights the moral and religious issues facing those who, after the initial wave of patriotic enlistment in the early months of the war, had to decide whether or not to enlist. Vialls had given long thought to enlisting, the popular speeches and lurid journalism of 1914 not having moved him, but by 1915 he was convinced of his duty and volunteered, even though he told the headmaster that he hated the idea of spilling blood and hoped to avoid it.

In mid-1915 the military situation was gloomy. Attacks on the Western Front in France had not made the hoped-for breakthroughs and the possibility of air strikes and of invasion, were the Germans to push forward, had to be taken seriously. In May 1915 an anti-aircraft hooter was installed at the electricity works, to be sounded by the

12

The swimming attendances of the long-distance boys have been exceedingly good. The town boys, in spite of their advantage, have not shown much keenness. By sports day, we hope to be able to show more than the average ability.

In the athletic sports there is every prospect of a good result, especially among the younger boys, who are very keen.   E.F.J.

✢ ✢ ✢

In Memoriam.
EDMUND VIALLS.
Born Feb. 20th, 1888.
Died June 30th, 1918.

"Tu ne quaesieris (scire nefas) quem mihi, quem tibi finem di dederint. . . . ut melius, quicquid erit, pati."
"Ask not ('twere wrong) what God has in store for me and what for you. It were better to bear the future, whatever it be."

These words from his beloved Horace were quoted by him on that last summer evening we spent together. I wonder now whether he realised how supremely fitting they are to his life. He applied them to a particular occasion, his last day in school, wondering in his heart what the future would bring him, yet perfectly willing to bear his lot. During five years of the closest and most intimate friendship, I have never known him grumble when things were going wrong, even the big things of his life. He was ever prepared to go on facing the difficulties, however great.

His life was given to service. He was never happier than when doing good turns, particularly if he had to go out of his way to do them. Nothing was too much trouble for him. Even a few hours before his death, he walked up to

13

his bed in the ward, thinking that he was saving someone else the trouble of carrying him.

He lived a clean and pure life and was absolutely straight in all his dealings, even to the minutest detail. Everything he did stood or fell by this one test—right. When the war broke out, he gave long and serious thought to the part he ought to play in it. Popular speeches and the superficial appeals of modern journalism in the autumn of 1914 grated on his finer feelings. His heart ached for the opportunity of shutting out the utter callousness of the whole matter, so that he might give thought to deciding on his particular duty. Once his mind was made up, he was satisfied that he must offer his services to his country. When he volunteered for the Army in 1915, he did so from sheer sense of duty, sense of right. But his soul shuddered at the very thought of shedding human blood, and he hoped against hope even to the end that he would be able to avoid such means.

In those long evening talks by the fireside, I had a unique opportunity of looking deeply into his soul. Then I found that his one purpose in life was to serve his Maker and to extend His Kingdom. He gave sober and serious thought to his religion and he was satisfied in his mind that he was in this world for the purpose of serving his God.

Let us "sorrow not, even as others which have no hope." His death was a triumph. We are the losers, the gain is Heaven's, for his was a beautiful soul.   T.

────────

AN APPRECIATION BY AN OLD COLLEAGUE.

Mr. L. S. Suggate writes: "As a colleague of his for nearly four years, I should like to testify to the extraordinary energy and enthusiasm he devoted to his work at the school. Those whom he taught had no means of knowing the time and labour he devoted independently of work in the school to make his teaching successful, though there are some with whom he worked privately who will remember with gratitude the interest he took in their careers. As a housemaster, he threw the same energy that he showed in all school activities into promoting that healthy keenness in the Surrey House that so often carried that house to

Obituary in the Dorking High School Magazine, summer term 1918, of schoolmaster Edmund Vialls (1888–1918) who joined up in 1915. The obituary highlights the moral and religious questions facing those who were not initially moved by unquestioning patriotism.

superintendent of police (on the orders of the chief constable) in order to warn inhabitants when enemy aircraft were in the vicinity. Its deployment was not successful, however. A practice use in early July was mistaken for a fire call, leading to a dispute between the fire chief and the superintendent of police. As a result, the chief constable was instructed by the council that the hooter was only to be used with the permission of the council and he was advised to arrange some other signal to warn of enemy aircraft, such as a whistle.

Invasion was a fear throughout Sussex, Kent and Surrey, from which direction an invasion might be expected to come. With much of

France and virtually all of Belgium under German control, there was always the possibility of an advance to the Channel should the Western powers' entrenched line of defence not hold. Defence of the southern counties was prepared for in detail by local defence committees. The Dorking Area Defence Committee had been founded on the outbreak of war under the Defence of the Realm Act 1914. A sub-committee had responsibility for the parishes of North and South Holmwood and Coldharbour (the village of Betchworth fell outside the Dorking committee's remit and into the Reigate area). The task of the area committee was to formulate a plan of action to be implemented in the event of invasion by the enemy. The first major task of the local defence committees was to compile a property-by-property list of all horses, cattle and sheep held in the area, and of motor cars and motorcycles, together with supplies of petrol, fodder and crops in the barns. Once the extent of property was established, plans could be made for the evacuation of everything that might be of assistance to the Kaiser's armies should invasion occur. It was envisaged that livestock from the Dorking area would be driven west and north, away from any invading army, together with all cars and motorcycles. Fodder, supplies of foodstuffs, petrol and useful tools were also to be evacuated, leaving nothing that might prove useful to the enemy (though it was not communicated to the inhabitants whether their possessions were to be requisitioned or paid for). Many of the horses listed, including those used by the fire brigade, were subsequently commandeered for military use, the lists prepared in order to plan the evacuation no doubt also providing the authorities with a handy guide to what was available for conscription into service.

Once the lists of livestock had been prepared, plans were drawn up by the various local committees in liaison with the Surrey Defence Committee (which was based in Caxton House in Westminster) for the route that such removals would take. Assuming that any attack would come from the south and east, it was agreed that 'clearances' would be driven into the heart of England towards Berkshire and Buckinghamshire. Each parish was required to prepare for this eventuality. Local defence committees therefore appointed drovers to accompany the animals and arranged the swearing-in of special constables so that there might be sufficient manpower with the authority to police the evacuation. It was envisaged that such chaos as

was likely to ensue would give rise to opportunities for fraud and theft, as well as to much human distress as animals were, sometimes forcibly, removed.

Cattle, horses and sheep from Dorking and the areas to the south were to be driven via Clandon Park, Sutton Place, Worplesden Common, Pirbright, Bisley Common and Bagshot Park to Windsor Great Park. Local animals would reach Clandon Park by travelling from Beare Green, through Holmwood and Dorking to Wotton and Abinger, where they would merge with incoming columns from other districts, proceeding towards Guildford. The route was amended in January 1915 by the military advisor to the local emergency committee, with animals to the south going via Stonebridge Road instead, then from Dorking via Ranmore to West Horsley. The plans were detailed. Assessments were made of the number of wagons required to transport the forage that would be needed en route, together with the matches, iron, horseshoes, anvils and grindstones that were not to be left to fall into enemy hands. Consideration was given to the need for shelter and water for the herds that would be passing through from Sussex and Kent, taking the same route thereafter as the Holmwood and Dorking herds, and for the needs of the slaughtermen who would have to accompany the animals. It was to have been a vast movement: all the livestock of the south-east of the country simultaneously on the march in a great movement of people and animals, cars, motorbikes, wagons and carts that would have clogged roads for days at a time, needing food, fuel, sanitary facilities and shelter as they went, no doubt with families joining the columns as people sought to remove themselves from the path of the advancing armies.

There was no general evacuation plan for human residents, though a sub-committee was formed, under the auspices of local vicars together with a number of local women, to compile lists of mothers with small children, the elderly and infirm who might require to be removed, while local vehicles were assessed regarding the number of passengers that they might carry away. With the removal of supplies of food and fuel, together with all means of transport, the remaining population would have faced such devastation as had been suffered by civilian populations many times over the preceding centuries in continental Europe.

Special constables were appointed in April 1915 to police the

potential evacuation. The men appointed were mainly farmers and bailiffs from the local farms. List-making continued as committees made enquiries as to the existence of firearms and ammunition in the area. However, the committees began to encounter resistance to their enquiries. Civilians were seeing increasing restrictions on their freedoms; licensing hours and regulations on lighting after dark were also met with mixed support.

Should the feared invasion come, the local defence corps were training in readiness. Villagers were encouraged by the High Sheriff of Surrey, Loe Strachey, to use rifle ranges to prepare themselves for the defence of their nation. In Newdigate the Reverend Bird advised those under and over age for recruitment to join the rifle club. 'That Gemany will endeavour to land some troops in England at some time or other is quite evident,' he wrote. 'Oostend, where some of her troops are at the moment, is not far from England.' A few trained men landed in England might do a lot of harm, he warned, and should Calais be taken they would 'be able to do much more than we imagine'.

In May the Newdigate Volunteer Company marched behind the village band through the village to a public meeting at the school room. Reverend Bird (whose own son had been killed three days earlier, though the news is unlikely to have reached his father by the day of the meeting) commented that the country was now not fighting for Belgium but for its very existence, that there remained hundreds and thousands of young men who would not be missed if they went to fight, and that everyone must do something if they were not to see the country extinct. There was much rivalry between villages: thirty had joined the volunteer training corps and Newdigate was urged not to be beaten by Capel but to recruit thirty-one.

In the summer of 1915 the local volunteer corps were called on to dig defensive trenches in Merstham for the protection of London and also to protect railway lines. Trainees camped at Box Hill and practised mock warfare. In July the 10th (Mid Surrey) Battalion paraded at Mickleham Hall and detachments from Dorking, Leatherhead, Ashtead, Cobham, Mickleham and Bookham practised for the August bank holiday parade at Denbies. On the bank holiday 4,000 men from local volunteer corps converged for the field day at Ranmore. They were billeted in schools and public buildings and undertook a mock defence of London (envisaging a route similar to that outlined in the fictional

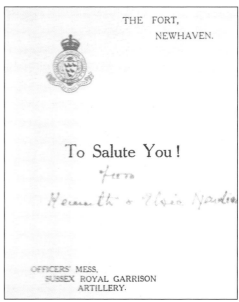

There was no respite from images of war, even at Christmas. This card was sent at Christmas 1915 to Felix Calvert of Ockley Court (a large mansion between Ockley and Capel). The sender was an officer of the Sussex Royal Garrison Artillery stationed in the Fort at Newhaven. Felix Calvert was a member of the Calvert family of Ockley Court. He was a child during the war. His aunt, Maud Calvert, had married Henry Cubitt, heir to Denbies, and was the mother of three boys killed in the war.

Battle of Dorking), with troops converging on Dorking from Burford and Netley. Crowds of spectators watched and afterwards the officers were invited to tea at Denbies; the troops were allowed to visit the gardens.

A decisive breakthrough against the heavily-defended German positions was needed in order to prevent German advances that might lead to the feared invasion. With the failure at Gallipoli to get to the Germans by the 'back door', all forces would now be concentrated on the Western Front. The warfare of 1915 had shown that more heavy artillery was needed, and more men to follow up initial attacks. However, the recruitment campaigns of 1915 had shown that voluntary enlistment could not be relied upon to provide those men.

Dorking Workhouse Hospital decorated for Christmas 1915. It is very much a wartime Christmas, with Union flags hung about the room and below pictures.

Do You Remember Suvla Bay, Sir?
Do you remember Suvla Bay, Sir?
Yes Lime Tree Gully and Anzac, too
Also the beach at Lalla Baba
Where the shrapnel often flew.

I remember the night we landed, Sir,
There were Turks there by the score,
And didn't their batteries paste us
As we waded to the shore.

But we landed in spite of it all, Sir,
And the Turks they turned and ran,
And we chased them over the hill, Sir,
British Bull Dogs to a man.

But then, a sad thing happened, Sir,
After facing death again and again,
We were forced to retire some miles, Sir,
For our reinforcements never came.

Then we entrenched ourselves, Sir,
Still feeling stiff and sore,
And we held the line right bravely,
But alas! advanced no more.

Then, water, it was scarce, Sir,
Till we found a Turkish well,
And their snipers they got going
And they made it a little Hell.

A poem on the Gallipoli campaign written by Driver P. Donovan of the 11th Signal Company, Royal Engineers, to his home in Dorking conveys the bitterness of a soldier who feels let down, seeing the bravery and lives of his comrades wasted.

M. Gilbert's War
On 3 July 1911 an aeroplane piloted by the Frenchman Monsieur Gilbert came down on Holmwood Common during the course of the Circuit of Europe air race. The race had begun on 18 June and Gilbert had been flying from Shoreham on the south coast to Hendon in North London when forced to land. In these early days of aviation,

Crowds surround M. Gilbert's plane at Holmwood Farm.

emergency landings were not uncommon: of fifty-two competitors in the race, only nine finished. Gilbert's plane was the only one to do so without major repairs.

The landing, on farmland at Holmwood Farm behind North Holmwood School, was quite an event for a district where most would never have seen a plane before. Monsieur Gilbert could not speak English and a chef was brought in from the Falkland Arms in Dorking to translate. Crowds turned out on the common, with bicycles and prams, to watch the spectacle. North Holmwood School's headmaster commented in his log that: 'many boys [were] absent this am owing to the fall of an aeroplane in the district.' Once repairs had been carried out, the plane was pulled from its resting place behind the school and up the hill past the church to the cricket field to take off again. Its wings had to be removed in order to manoeuvre it up the bends and gradients.

People in Holmwood and Dorking would no doubt have thought fondly of that pre-war summer day when reading of M. Gilbert's fate in the *Sunday Pictorial* of 4 July 1915. Gilbert had been flying planes for the French military since the outbreak of war, but his military flying career came to an end in July 1915. After attacking the German Zeppelin sheds at Friedrichshafen, he was forced to land in Switzerland where he was interned by the neutral Swiss. Having sworn to avenge the death of his friend M. Garros – his plane was named the Avenger – M. Gilbert was reportedly led to internment, weeping at no longer being able to serve his country.

Local woman Nelly Upfold recorded M. Gilbert's later fate on the back of the photographs she kept of the day a plane came down in Holmwood.

Mr Vanderbilt and the *Lusitania*

American multi-millionaire Alfred Gwynne Vanderbilt (1877–1915) spent as much time in Britain before the war as he did in the United States, much of it in the Dorking area.

One of the wealthiest men in the world, Vanderbilt was the second son of Cornelius Vanderbilt II, whose family had made a fortune in the United States' railway boom. When Cornelius died in 1899 (having disinherited his first son), he left the best part of his

fortune to the 22-year-old Alfred, who is thought to have inherited some $70 million.

Vanderbilt came from an Anglophile family. His cousin, Consuelo, was married to Charles Spencer-Churchill, 9th Duke of Marlborough, who had long-standing connections in the Dorking area. (The duke had spent some of his youth in the 1870s at Oakdene in Holmwood and his American stepmother, Lily, the Dowager Duchess, had rented Deepdene, between Holmwood and Dorking, until her death in 1911.)

Horse-and-carriage racing was Alfred Vanderbilt's passion. Along the various roads to the south coast he was often to be seen running his carriages at great speed to and

Alfred Gwynne Vanderbilt.

from London in recreation of the great days of coach travel before the advent of the railways. On these excursions his guard would be attired in a gold-braided red coat and top hat. For the Holmwood stretch of the route Vanderbilt had a particular fondness; his coachman would blow his horn in advance to bring out local children in the hope of pennies or sweets.

Vanderbilt's coach and horses outside the Burford Bridge Hotel at the foot of Box Hill before 1914.

Vanderbilt had a colourful private life. He was divorced by his first wife on the grounds of his adultery with the wife of the Cuban ambassador in London. In 1912 he married Margaret Emerson McKim, who was living in Betchworth. She had also been married before and when she divorced her first husband on grounds of cruelty Vanderbilt had faced a lawsuit on account of 'alienation' of McKim's wife's affections. Just four witnesses attended the private wedding ceremony in Reigate.

On 1 May 1915 Alfred Vanderbilt left New York on the *Lusitania* for a meeting of the International Horse Breeders Association in London. He was also to have offered a fleet of wagons to the British Red Cross. Only days before, Germany had issued warnings that all British ships in Atlantic waters should consider themselves at risk of attack. Vanderbilt received an anonymous personal warning not to travel but laughed it off as a prank to discomfort him. On the seventh day of the voyage the *Lusitania* was sunk by a torpedo.

For days the family waited for news at the Vanderbilt Hotel in New York. When none came, Vanderbilt's sister, Gertrude Whitney (the sculptor and founder of the Whitney Museum) telegrammed for help from her brother-in-law in England, Almeric Paget. (Later Lord Queensbury, Paget was married to Gertrude's husband's sister and they had been living at Deepdene for a while.)

German notice to neutral American travellers warning them against crossing the Atlantic on British ships in April 1915, as printed in the New York Times. By coincidence Alfred Vanderbilt's uncle, George, had had a ticket to sail on the Titanic but had not travelled when his mother had a premonition of disaster. His luggage had not been unloaded and went down with the ship. (Photo courtesy of The Lusitania Resource)

NOTICE!

TRAVELLERS intending to embark on the Atlantic voyage are reminded that a state of war exists between Germany and her allies and Great Britain and her allies; that the zone of war includes the waters adjacent to the British Isles; that, in accordance with formal notice given by the Imperial German Government, vessels flying the flag of Great Britain, or of any of her allies, are liable to destruction in those waters and that travellers sailing in the war zone on ships of Great Britain or her allies do so at their own risk.

IMPERIAL GERMAN EMBASSY
WASHINGTON, D. C., APRIL 22, 1915.

Vanderbilt's body was never recovered. Aged 38 when he died, he left a son by his first wife and two infants by his second. In the immediate aftermath of the sinking, lurid stories were printed in the papers recounting acts of bravery that seem to have been invented by journalists. Nonetheless, eyewitness testimony seems to suggest that Vanderbilt did assist child passengers into lifeboats and that he probably did give up his life-jacket, even though he could not swim. The *Dorking and Leatherhead Advertiser* wrote that: 'People will not talk of Mr Vanderbilt in future as the millionaire sportsman and man of pleasure. He will be remembered as the "Children's Hero" and men and women will salute his name.'

Vanderbilt's roadside memorial, beside the northbound A24 between Mid and South Holmwood, was erected by his friends from the British Horse Society. It sits on land now owned by the National Trust which has been provided with a small fund for its maintenance. The inscription reads:

In memory of Alfred Gwynne Vanderbilt
A gallant gentleman and fine sportsman who perished in the *Lusitania* May 7th 1915.
This stone erected on his favourite road by a few of his British coaching friends and admirers.

The Vanderbilt Memorial.

Ralph Vaughan Williams: the Composer in Wartime

The composer and folk song collector Ralph Vaughan Williams (1872–1958) grew up at Leith Hill Place, the home of his grandmother, Caroline Wedgwood (nee Darwin). After attending Charterhouse he studied composition at the Royal College of Music and then went to Cambridge. He then lived in London but kept a room at Leith Hill Place, which his mother Margaret inherited in 1911. From there he was able to pursue the collection of local folk songs and to participate in the Leith Hill Musical Competitions.

Ralph Vaughan Williams.

The Leith Hill Musical Competition, in which all the local village choirs took part, was founded by his sister Margaret (Meggie) and Evangeline (Eva), Lady Farrer, of Abinger Hall in 1904. Vaughan Williams conducted the first competition at the Public Halls on West Street in May 1905 and went on to bring his eminent musical friends down to participate. The composer Gustav Holst came in 1909 as an adjudicator and Hubert Parry presented the awards in 1911. However, in 1914 it was announced that the competition would be cancelled for the duration of the war.

Although he was over the age of 40 when the war began, Ralph Vaughan Williams enlisted, first with the special constabulary and then with the Royal Army Medical Corps. Eschewing a commission, he took on the lowly position of wagon orderly. In 1915 his unit was billeted in Dorking for three months. He was, reported contemporaries, very ungainly in khaki and was taunted by the 'wags'. He was not suited to the regimentation of army life. Lifelong friend Henry Steggles from his RAMC days records that:

> I gradually found myself helping him when in billets, with his equipment, for his cap was never straight, even when 'chin-straps will be worn'; if it was, his cap-badge was all askew, his puttees were his nightmare and so I believe I lent a hand to ensure that he went on parade, to quote his own words, in a 'correct and soldier-like' manner.

Steggles remembers the composer on the route marches to Guildford and back as a fit man, apart from his flat feet, who slouched and suffered much without complaint. On one occasion when the unit went to church parade he played the organ, selecting a popular song called *Make your mind up, Maggie MacKenzie*, somewhat disguised, as the men took their seats. On another occasion he agreed to act as organist if he could be supplied with a volunteer choir from the unit. Choir and organist were marched to the church under command of an officer. Once there, Vaughan Williams appeared to forget he was in the army and commanded officer, sergeant and men in the same manner.

Later in his military service Vaughan Williams formed a band with instruments bought from the profits of the canteen plus donations. However, he did not take part in divisional concert parties or theatre, which would have seen him excused other duties, saying that they were doing well enough without him. Alan Piper, later a school headmaster in Dorking, told his pupils that while in France leading a platoon of men he had met Dr Vaughan Williams walking along a French road, weary and with a large hole in his sock. Knowing that he was a famous musician, he had felt humble to see him 'doing his bit'.

Vaughan Williams served as a stretcher-bearer in France and Salonika. In December 1917 he was commissioned as a second lieutenant in the Royal Garrison Artillery, and prolonged exposure to gunfire began a process of hearing loss that led to profound deafness in old age. In 1918 he was appointed Director of Music, First Army.

Vaughan Williams returned to Dorking in the 1920s, taking up residence at The White Gates on Westcott Road, where he lived into old age.

John Stavridi and Greek Neutrality

John Stavridi (later Sir John) lived at Ferndale on Mill Road between Holmwood and Blackbrook. Brought up in Britain of Greek parents and trained as a lawyer, he was a director of the British-owned Ionian Bank which operated in the eastern Mediterranean. He was also the consul-general for Greece in London.

In November 1915 Stavridi was sent by the British government on a secret mission to Greece to persuade the Greeks not to hold strictly to their policy of neutrality in the conflict. Had they done so, British and allied troops retreating through Greece after the failure of the Gallipoli campaign would have been disarmed and interned. Such troops were desperately needed on the Western Front. Though King Constantine I is often said to have had German sympathies, he had rebuffed efforts from Germany as well as from Britain and France to come into the war. Stavridi's mission was to force Greece to favour the allied cause. When diplomatic efforts failed, he threatened a naval blockade of the country's coastline and the confiscation of its merchant fleet, which would have devastated the nation's economy.

Many in Greece regarded Stavridi's actions as traitorous, viewing him as putting the interests of Britain above those of Greece, whose neutrality was threatened. He was forced to resign his position as consul. However, Stavridi was convinced that the Western allies would win the war and that Greek cooperation would be in her long-term interests. In 1917 internal conflict over Greece's alignment in the war became almost civil war, and Constantine was forced into exile. His son Alexander was appointed king in his place. Stavridi was reappointed to his position in 1917, with the restoration of a government sympathetic to the allies. He went on to arrange the chartering of Greek merchant vessels for the Western powers. After the war he was knighted by the British government.

CHAPTER 4

1916: Conscription, Exemption and Objection

Conscription was introduced by the Military Service Act 1916. A year and a half into the war the French army was in need of relief and it was clear that the British army would need more men if there was to be any chance of the planned summer offensives pushing the Germans back from their entrenched positions in France and Belgium. Despite the targeting of potential recruits made possible by national registration, voluntary schemes had failed to produce enough recruits. In January 1916 conscription was applied to all unmarried men between the ages of 18 and 41. In June of the same year it was extended to married men, save those who were widowed with dependent children. (The age limit was eventually raised to 51.) Ministers of the church remained exempt from service.

With service no longer voluntary, schools and parishes ceased to publish lists of those serving. These had served as an example and an encouragement to those remaining behind, but were now no longer necessary.

Conscription was administered locally. Appeals against conscription could be made to local Military Service Act Tribunals on the grounds that the appellant was doing civilian work of national importance, that his conscription would cause domestic hardship, on grounds of ill health, or of conscientious objection. The tribunals were able to grant temporary or conditional exemptions. It was left to individual councils'

discretion how they constituted the local tribunals and how they selected members. In Dorking it was agreed that the various interests of the district, as well as the national interest, should be represented. The local branch of the National Union of Railwaymen stressed it was imperative that the working classes should be represented, which was agreed, and a seven-man committee was put into place. It transpired that as many men appealed to tribunals as went willingly into the army.

Dorking was an agricultural area with much of the population engaged in food production or related trades, and initially farm workers tended to be allowed exemption from military service. Other employers and tradesmen struggled to prevent their staff, without whom they could not run their businesses, being called up. Applications were made to the Dorking Military Tribunal for exemptions on behalf of butchers, bakers, shop staff, timber-fellers and woodworkers, headmasters and voluntary firemen. Albert Turner of the White Hart Inn at Beare Green tried to hang on to his cab drivers. Landowners, such as Colonel Henry Helsham-Jones of Redlands near Holmwood and Cuthbert Heath of Anstie Grange, applied to exempt their gamekeepers and chauffeurs.

In the early days of conscription, exemptions were given for a wide variety of occupations considered vital to the nation: rag-and-bone men, road haulage carriers, steam-roller drivers and timber-fellers. In particular, conditional exemptions were freely given to all agricultural trades, as the importance of food production to the war effort was recognized. Carters, bakers, agricultural labourers, cow-keepers, farmers and even smallholders such as the community at Cudworth in Newdigate were awarded exempt status. However, over time the occupations went from starred exemptions to conditional exemptions to being required to serve. Men repeatedly came before the tribunal as they moved jobs or their employment was reclassified as being of less importance as the demand for men at the front remained unsatisfied. Even those exempted were required to join the local defence volunteers (unless, like Arthur Piper, the bailiff at Inholms Farm at Blackbrook, they were adjudged to have no time for such service).

The work of the tribunal would always be controversial: who it exempted and who it sent for military service was open to scrutiny and debate. In September 1916 Alfred Dean of Dean's stores in Newdigate wrote from France complaining to the *Dorking and Leatherhead Advertiser* of the exempt status of Joseph Sanders, a single 36-year-

old coachman at the stables of Mrs Janson at Newdigate Place. Sanders, despite having no dependants and no business, had obtained an exemption, whereas Mr Dean, a married man over 40 who was running a vital business as grocer, baker, ironmonger, corn, meal and general store (most of whose employees were already in the services), had been refused an exemption. Was it right, he asked, that the state now need support his wife when there were single men still not serving? A rejoinder was published, claiming that the coachman was in fact also driving the engine for electric light at Newdigate Place, being the only man left in the stables and engine room of an employer who had lost twenty employees to the services since the outbreak of war.

Some who might, on the face of it, not seem to be doing work of national importance, were deemed to be doing so. Early in 1917 the town solicitor Mr W.J. Down asked for a conditional exemption for his clerk, Ernest Sellick. Aged 37 (and living at 8 Norfolk Road), Sellick had been rejected as medically unfit in November 1916 and January 1917. In June 1917 he was passed as fit. Mr Down protested that Sellick had been employed at Down's for twenty years and had the entire management of the business under his supervision, including such vital areas as the magistrates court, land leasing, administration of the local National Registration scheme, various committees for the council, and the operation of the Military Tribunal itself. A copying clerk could be replaced but someone with Sellick's experience could not. As his duties were of national importance in contributing to the war effort, exemption was sought on the grounds that Sellick was indispensible. One of the partners and two clerks had already joined up, and apart from one clerk who had been medically rejected, the firm employed no-one else of military age. The tribunal's military representative agreed that Sellick was indispensible and ordered a temporary exemption until June 1917. By June the following year Down claimed that the situation was worse and that Sellick was now employed solely on local authority work. Were Sellick to go, he said, the business would be reduced to an office boy and a 'girl'. It was agreed that Sellick was doing work of more importance than if he was to go into the army because of the heavy workload now being undertaken by local authorities. He retained his exemption throughout the war.

Few came before the Dorking Military Tribunal claiming

conscientious objection (the number was only 2 per cent nationally), but those who did appear to have had their supporters in the community. E.W. Turner of Holmwood was exempted on conscientious grounds as long as he did work of national importance and so contributed to the war effort. He was offered work by the local lay preacher, Mr Isemonger, who had a walking stick and umbrella-handle factory near the Norfolk Arms on the road to Horsham. That proposal was rejected by the tribunal, which instead required Turner to work at a flour mill in Ewell. Umbrella handles and walking sticks were perhaps not vital to the war economy. However, it also seems the tribunal felt that there ought to be an effort or hardship, or possibly punishment, inflicted on those who were granted conscientious objector status. Frederick Pethick-Lawrence of Holmwood, the women's suffrage campaigner (and later Labour MP), was also denied the chance to take a job locally at Wattlehurst Farm in Capel when awarded exempt status; he too was forced to travel out of the area to work in Sussex. Other conscientious objectors included the socialist John Aitcheson, who before the war had set up summer camps at Cudworth in Newdigate that were used by Labour youth organizations.

As a last resort, some men simply disappeared. The *Dorking and Leatherhead Advertiser* carried half-page advertisements listing men who had failed to appear for military service with their last known addresses, requesting information from the reading public as to their whereabouts.

With many men of military age engaged in work of importance, high levels of ill health and unfitness in the general population and tens of thousands on conditional exemptions, the numbers raised by conscription fell short of those achieved voluntarily earlier in the war. As time went on, standards for service were lowered for volunteers and conscripts. Holmwood School's headmaster, Stephen Bowring, was accepted into the army in March 1916, despite having been rejected on four previous attempts to enlist because of his defective eyesight, and Kenneth Harman Young was rejected on failing two medicals before being accepted into the Civil Service Rifles in November 1916.

Men like Bowring and Young were anxious to play their part and many who were rejected worried that they would 'miss out', but two years into the war people were used to seeing newspaper columns every week listing the dead, wounded and missing, so it is not surprising that

many were reluctant to join up. The Somme offensive, necessary to take pressure off the French who were in danger of being overcome at Verdun, saw a shocking increase in the casualty lists. Vicars' addresses in parish magazines no longer lamented the loss of the odd man; throughout the Somme offensive the names mentioned in editorials came thick and fast. December 30th's issue of the *Dorking and Leatherhead Advertiser* listed seventy names from the district – from Dorking to Ockley, Newdigate and Peaslake – who had been killed in 1916. In the town alone the Somme offensive, between July and November, claimed twenty-eight lives, eight being lost on the first day.

Reports of deaths and short obituaries were now so commonplace that they were taking up too much space in the local paper. On the death of the Hon. Alick Cubitt, son of Henry Cubitt, in late 1917, the editor commented that the *Advertiser* would like to have been able to give public recognition to the parents of all who died, but space only permitted them to give it to prominent figures. Similarly the Dorking British School annual report opined that, with twenty-four former pupils killed by the end of 1917: 'the name of each who had laid down his life is worthy of more than the simple record, but our space does not permit.' Nonetheless, the editor was able to find some words of encouragement for his readers: 'Though during the year the school has often been saddened, and also robbed of its joy through the overshadowing of many of its homes by sorrow and death, yet the spirit of courage and of fidelity to duty has not failed.'

SURREY AND THE WAR.

TRANSPORT DRIVER'S DEATH.

Mrs. Salmon, of Hart Gardens, Dorking, has received the sad news of the death of her husband in France. He was a motor transport driver, and has died in hospital from a fractured skull. The circumstances by which he met with his injuries are not yet known. Mr. Salmon before joining the Army was employed at the wine stores of Messrs. H. G. Kingham and Co. His widow is left with a young baby.

PTE. F. J. WELLS
(City of London Regiment).

Mr. and Mrs. W. Wells, Pixham-lane, Dorking, have received the sad news of the death in action of their eldest son, Pte. Frederick James Wells, who had been previously reported wounded. He joined the Army two months after the war broke out. He was an old National School boy, and was 23 years of age.

Death notices, 1916. The weekly paper carried notices of this type regularly, with round-ups coinciding with major offensives.

However, for local authorities, the dead were less problematic than the living. In November the council discussed fears that not enough provision was being made for the inevitable wave of disabled soldiers who would return to England if current casualty rates continued. National government had taken no responsibility, so it would be down

to local rate-payers to support the injured and their families. A sub-committee was formed to propose a plan of action.

By mid-1916 Dorking and the villages had seen the departure of regular troops, the territorials and reservists, voluntary enlistment and the beginning of conscription. So many men from Holmwood were either in France or appointed special constables that the local Defence Committee reported difficulties in finding any men to appoint to drive animals out of the area in the event of invasion. Civilian businesses struggled to recruit and retain staff from the reduced pool of working-age men available. Despite the exemption of men needed for food production, there was not enough casual labour in the area to bring in the harvest and older children were granted exemption from school attendance so that they could undertake farm work. At the great estates and grand houses the diversion of male labour into the military or work of national importance, and of female labour into male roles, saw gardens untended and houses neglected, many never to return to their former glory.

Most leisure pursuits had been curtailed by the war. Sporting societies had ceased competing, although occasionally a cricket match

Certificate, St Paul's School. As a consequence of the shortages of war the school gave out certificates rather than prizes.

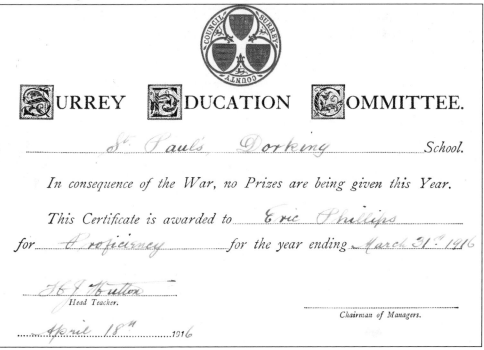

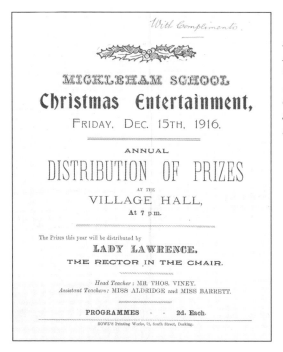

With Compliments.

Programme for the Mickleham School Christmas entertainment, 1916. One of the entertainments was a song about wartime housewives.

would be organized with an ad hoc team to play against visiting troops. Leith Hill Tower, once visited by thousands on bank holidays, now saw war casualties signing their names in the visitors' book (although these must have been reasonably healthy, given the steepness of the climb). In early summer Corporal Lasseter RAMC from the Kitchener Hospital, Brighton, and Captain Casemore, Sergeant Pullen and Sergeant Bamfield of the Royal Engineers from the war hospital in Croydon came on day trips. In May three members of Torpedo Boat Crew 076 looked south towards the sea, and in June members of the 4th Canadian Siege Battery and the 2nd Welsh Regiment visited.

In schools there was a constant turnover of teachers, and children were sent home for lack of staff. Mr Cousin, headmaster of the Dorking British School, described the school as operating at 'War Strength' with his teaching responsibilities now leaving little time for general supervision, and he admitted that school work was taking unusual forms. South Holmwood School lost two headmasters to the army. It had engaged a temporary female head teacher in 1914 and employed another, Lucy Strudwick, in May 1916. She saw the school through to

Dorking ladies' cricket team and Anzacs from a hospital at Epsom. In September 1916 the ladies played the Anzacs on the Cotmandene. The match was eight-a-side and the Anzacs were handicapped by having to bat and bowl reverse-handed. The Anzacs were duly bowled out for 24, and the ladies won by 11 runs. A collection was taken for St Dunstan's Hostel for Blind Soldiers and Sailors. Tea at The Bungalow was followed by a night of music and song.

Another cricket match between a Dorking team and visiting Anzacs. Seated centre in the second row up (in black) is Canon Chichester of St Martin's Church, and to his right is Dr Blakeney, Dorking's most committed recruiter.

The Worrow family of the Norfolk Arms Hotel at Mid Holmwood, just south of Dorking. Maggie Worrow, pictured to the rear of the cart, took over the running of a large business and the treasurership of the Ancient Order of Foresters when her husband left for the army. (Photo courtesy of Eileen Fox)

the return of the permanent headmaster at the end of the war. Of necessity, women took over the running of areas of life from which they would previously have been excluded. Maggie Worrow, wife of the landlord of the Norfolk Arms Hotel on the road south of Dorking, took on the role of treasurer to the local branch of the Ancient Order of Foresters (as well as running the business) when her husband was called up.

The composer Ralph Vaughan Williams was surprised to find a 17-year-old female General Post Office worker installing a telephone extension in his room at Leith Hill Place. Ann Stewart had been employed to repair subscribers' phones when there were no men available to do the job. 'How did she like doing a man's job?' asked the composer. 'Very much,' replied Ann, for she got to meet so many interesting people. Thus the war changed what was considered acceptable or even possible for women, as young women like Ann found themselves out, unchaperoned, meeting people in an official and skilled capacity.

The wedding of Theresa Spencer of Stockrydons in Beare Green to James Clare, on 15 July 1916 at Holmwood. Theresa's brother-in-law Herbert Mason is in uniform. (Photo courtesy of Jayne Simms)

Mrs and Miss Turner had themselves photographed in their working outfits in 1916 when they were undertaking 'war work' with a butcher's on the High Street.

The Simms family at Stockrydons in Beare Green posing for a family photograph (with the pet cat) sent to a family member who was serving in France. (Photo courtesy of Jayne Simms)

Women also began to take on work on the land. The War Agricultural Service for Women was formed to mobilize women when food shortages (and price rises) were experienced as imports declined. With less food coming in to the country, it was necessary to produce more food with a reduced male workforce. The villages appointed registrars to recruit women for land work. However, many were sceptical: a farmer's wife from Newdigate with experience of farm work wrote to the paper: 'Woe betide England if the land falls to women to cultivate!' Mrs Cox of Blanks Farm suggested that town women, rather than being sent onto the land, should stay in town and instead replace the shop, office and factory workers who could then be spared for the front. Constance Aston of Sondes Place, who was the Dorking Rural District Council representative on the Surrey Committee for Women and Farm Labour, disagreed. She advocated women working the land rather than young boys as the practice of excusing absence from school in order to work on the farms was depriving the boys of their education.

Certificate presented to Eric Phillips of Dorking by the Overseas Club, Empire Day 1916, in recognition of his contributions towards collections for the troops fighting overseas. The Overseas Club encouraged children to bring in pennies to contribute to 'comforts' (particularly cigarettes and pipe tobacco) for the troops.

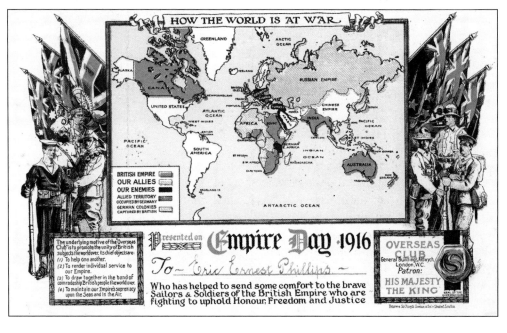

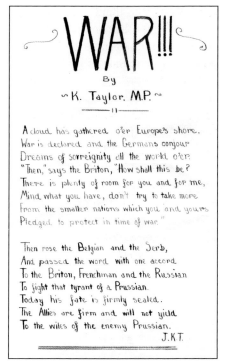
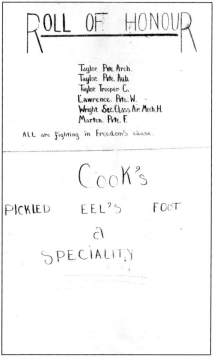

Handwritten poem from a Christmas journal written by schoolboy Kenneth Taylor. The poem appears in the schoolboy's magazine Our Own edition of Christmas 1916, edited by Taylor, a 13-year-old living at Lincoln Road. Taylor attended Dorking High School. On the back is a roll of honour listing those who were 'fighting in Freedom's cause', together with a mock advertisement, in imitation of school journals and parish magazines. It is not clear whether these were family members who were in the services or imaginary names.

Even the war effort could be hampered by lack of labour, however. In 1916 the War Office, when requisitioning timber from the nearby woods, demanded that the Rural District Council keep the bridle path to the Vaughan Williams' family farm at High Ashes clear of obstruction. The council replied that work was delayed because they could not get the horses and were short of men.

The effect on children of the lack of men in a world where all figures of authority were male was cause for comment. In November the *Dorking and Leatherhead Advertiser* ran a piece on 'restlessness' in schools, putting the problem down to the loss of well-trained

teachers and fathers, plus a loss of peers as older children were taken out of school to work in place of absent menfolk. Teachers were lost to budget cuts as well as to the war, as local authorities struggled to pay for services. In April 1916 Surrey County Council ordered reductions in staff numbers at some schools. St Paul's School in Dorking lost a class, the children having to be distributed around other classes.

Children's attendance at school was also more sporadic than it had been before the war as they took time off to see relatives on leave from the front, to help with short-handed businesses and to help in the fields. Before and during the war many pupils left school, mostly of necessity to work, before the age of 14. This increased during the war as children left school early to work in family businesses (where adult males had gone into the services), or were excused their studies to undertake farm work. In many local families the additional wage brought home by a working child was very welcome. From July 1916 older boys who were on school rolls could be granted agricultural exemptions from the requirement to attend. However, schools had to make applications to the County Council for them and exempted boys were recorded on school registers as absent which, as income was linked to attendance, affected a school's income. Monetary shortages were already affecting education: in June 1916 the headmaster at St Paul's School was informed that no reading books, textbooks or publications in general, pictures, maps, diagrams, science apparatus, chemicals, material for watercolour work or papers for chalk-work were to be requisitioned until further notice. Such restrictions made anything but a very basic education impossible.

Voluntary organizations such as the Ancient Order of Foresters, which ran most of what would now be provided by local councils in the way of social and emergency services, also struggled. Though many men of military age remained in the area in reserved occupations, they were drilling with the volunteer corps in their free time and therefore unable to give their time to the community. Older men were often working as special constables or volunteering in capacities related to the war effort. On the outbreak of war the Holmwood voluntary fire brigade lost several firemen who signed up to become special constables and were put on duty guarding bridges. By mid-1916 it had only one fireman available. Applications were made to the Dorking

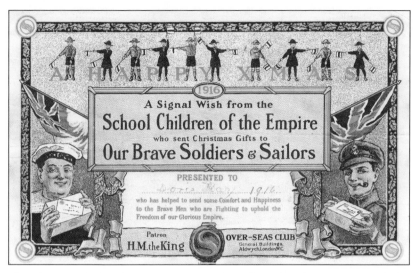

Certificate presented to Doris Kay of Dorking by the Overseas Club, Christmas 1916, in recognition of her contributions towards collections for the troops fighting overseas.

Military Tribunal for exemptions from military service for Chief Fire Officer Secretan and engineers Mercer and Worsfold. The applications were refused. The hooter was removed from the fire station and the telegraph office told that the service was no longer operating, leaving homes and businesses with no fire service closer than Dorking, a cycle ride away. Eventually a reserve brigade of men over military age or with exempt status was formed once the threat of invasion was considered unlikely and many of the special constables were stood down later in the year.

By the winter of 1916 there were obvious food shortages. From Newdigate F.E. Green wrote to the paper to suggest that the local Smith's Charity make grants of food available to pensioners whose purchasing power had dropped with the rise in prices. There was also a shortage of coal as the needs of the army competed with civilian demand for fuel for heating. In Holmwood holly was allocated for burning. Germany's campaign of submarine warfare and the disruption at the Channel ports resulted in a reduction in food imports from the United States, the Empire and Europe, and farming was affected by

The Holmwood voluntary fire brigade was formed in 1911 after a disastrous farm fire. Holmwood was too far away for cycle messengers to call out the Dorking brigade before a fire took hold. It was forced to disband in 1916 after conscription of the engineers and chief fire officer left only one volunteer fireman available.

lack of suitable manpower. Queues formed for essentials like butter, sugar and cheese, with shop owners attempting to apply a form of rationing by only allowing people to take a certain amount. William Dinnage recalls people queuing to buy their supplies and then returning to the back of the queue to appear again, this time hatted, in the hope of fooling the shop staff. Lady Laura Hampton of Oakdale opened a soup kitchen in Holmwood, and common-based activities such as charcoal-burning, long abandoned as unproductive and uncompetitive, reappeared in areas like Holmwood and Holmbury. Henry Cubitt announced that he would support the installation of pigstyes at allotments near Denbies to enable people to keep pigs and would allow the keeping of chickens there too. Under the Defence of the Realm Act 1914, under-utilized land could be commandeered for conversion to allotments in order to increase food production, but allotments had to be worked, thus putting more pressure on labour.

The threat of invasion had diminished by the end of 1916 as the Germans failed to push forward. However, increased enemy activity on the seas now threatened famine, bringing the war directly into Dorking homes.

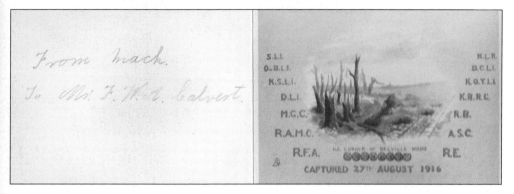

This card was sent to Felix Calvert of Ockley Court at Christmas 1916. It features Delville Wood, on the Somme, which was the site of fierce fighting between July and September of that year. A tactical success in securing the British army's right flank after the Somme offensive, the Battle of Delville Wood was hard-fought with many casualties on both sides. The experiences of the troops there have been described by Robert Graves in his autobiography, Goodbye to All That.

Staff at the Dorking Isolation Hospital in Logmore Lane, Westcott, during the war.

The Holmbury St Mary Prisoner of War Camp

In March 1916 an internment camp was established at Holmbury St Mary to the south-west of the town. About 1,000 enemy alien civilians were interned there. The camp was guarded by the Royal Defence Corps, which had been founded in 1916 and incorporated soldiers considered unsuitable for the front. The prisoners, dressed in grey uniforms with soft caps, worked at felling fir trees for timber that was taken to sawmills at the top of the Glade and by the school. A light railway transported timber to the pits. Beattie Ede later recalled that as a child she and the other children loved to play in the huge mounds of sawdust left after the prisoners had returned to camp but, although the prisoners were quiet and inoffensive (and clever woodworkers), they were not allowed to talk to them.

Guards at the Holmbury St Mary Prisoner of War Camp.

Despair and Suicide

Son of a Newdigate gamekeeper living at Henfold, Cook's Mate 2nd Class Westley Johns was named after a rifle. Like two of his brothers he joined the Royal Navy and while serving at the Royal Navy Barracks in Portsmouth in January 1916, he hanged himself at the age of 18. News reports suggest he had been afraid that he was to

be invalided out on account of a bad foot, but the coroner recorded him as being of 'unsound mind'.

Suicide took a toll on local men. In October 1916 Sergeant Thomas Trueman Chester of the Royal Defence Corps in Dorking was found shot through the head at the Rural District Council's headquarters in Harrow Road. He was 45 years old, was born and lived in Dorking, and had formerly served with the Queen's (Royal West Surrey) Regiment. The investigating authorities concluded that there was not sufficient evidence to determine whether his injuries were intentional or accidental, but it seems likely that he had taken his own life. Officialdom was willing to give him the benefit of the doubt.

A few months earlier, Holmwood gardener Victor Tickner, serving with the Royal Navy at Portsmouth, had cut his throat in a fit of insanity. After the war it was unanimously agreed by the Holmwood War Memorial Committee that his death occurred when on military service, and that notwithstanding the fact that he had taken his own life, his name should appear on the Holmwood memorial. Chester's name appears on the St Martin's and town war memorials.

In all cases the authorities seem to have preferred to ascribe the deaths to accident or unsoundness of mind, rather than intention caused by despair.

Boy Soldiers: Valentine 'Joe' Strudwick and Aubrey Hudson
Dorking's youngest military casualty in the First World War is often said to have been Joe Strudwick who was killed at the age of 15 years and 11 months on 14 January 1916.

Strudwick was born in Falkland Road on 14 February 1900 and so named Valentine, though he was known as Joe. He later moved with his gardener father, laundress mother and siblings to Orchard Road. After leaving St Paul's School he probably worked for his uncle, a coal merchant, and in other manual work. He must have lied about his age when he enlisted in January 1915 as he was only 14 years old. He joined 8th Battalion the Rifle Brigade and died near Ypres a year later.

The report of the boy's death in the *Dorking and Leatherhead*

Commemorative scroll in memory of Valentine 'Joe' Strudwick.

The grave of Valentine Strudwick at Essex Farm Cemetery near Ypres. The grave is one of the most visited of British war graves, partly because of the misapprehension that Strudwick was the youngest British soldier to lose his life in the war, and partly as he lies in the graveyard to the Essex Farm Field Hospital where John McCrae wrote In Flanders Fields, a much-visited site. His grave is often decked with commemorative crosses, poppies and soft toys.

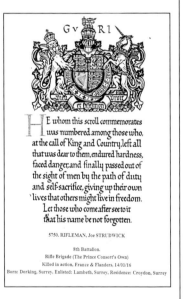

Advertiser on 22 January 1916 seeks not to question how a boy of such youth came to be serving but uses his example to shame reluctant older men into joining up. The piece also reveals how both press and officers were keen to report death as instantaneous and painless for the public back home:

Another Dorking lad has achieved honour by laying down his life for his country.

Pte. Valentine Joe Strudwick, of the 8th Rifle Brigade, joined up twelve months ago last January, and at the time of his death, on Jan.14th he had not reached his sixteenth birthday, he having been born on St. Valentine's Day, 1900.

His mother would naturally have liked to have kept him out of the Army for at least a year or two, but young Strudwick would not have it – a fine example to those of maturer years who have not yet joined, and perhaps a reproach?

With only six week's training the lad was sent over to France. Within a short time he lost two of his chums who were standing next to him – both instantaneously killed. The shock was such, with the addition of being badly gassed, that he was sent home and was for three months in hospital at Sheerness. On recovering he rejoined his regiment in France, and this week his mother received the following letter from his commanding officer, dated Jan.15th:

I am very sorry indeed to have to inform you that your son was killed by a shell on Jan. 14th. His death was quite instantaneous and painless and his body was carried by his comrades to a little cemetery behind the lines, where it was reverently buried this morning. A cross is being made and will shortly be erected on his grave. Rifleman Strudwick had earned the goodwill and respect of his comrades and his officers, and we are very sorry indeed to lose so good a soldier. On their behalf as well as my own I offer you sincere sympathy.

The deceased was Mrs Strudwick's second surviving son, and her grief is the greater because of the fact that she had not been able to see him since he joined the Army. She has another son in the Royal Field Artillery.

Young Strudwick was an old St. Paul's boy.

Valentine Strudwick is often claimed to be the youngest rifleman killed in the First World War (and this is often mistakenly taken to mean that he was the youngest serving soldier to have been killed). On this account his grave at Essex Farm Cemetery is much visited. Recent research, however, suggests that he was not the youngest rifleman killed, nor was he the youngest local casualty.

Aubrey Hudson of Newdigate died on 28 July 1916 at just 15 years and 1 month. He had not been much of a scholar, being repeatedly punished in 1913 and 1914 at Newdigate School for inattention, for being 'generally slack', for talking, and for careless writing and spelling. His last punishment was in September 1914,

just after war had broken out. Perhaps he could no longer see the point of school; perhaps the army seemed to offer a release from the punishments of school; or perhaps his family needed the money. Contemporaries suggest that he joined up immediately, but even if he did not join up until early 1915, he could have been no older than 13 when he began serving with the 22nd Battalion Royal Fusiliers. By Christmas 1915, still aged only 14, he was in France. He died on the Somme, going missing in action at Delville Wood, one of the bloodiest engagements of the war. So numerous were the dead being reported home at this point in the war that the *Dorking and Leatherhead Advertiser* did not even run an obituary piece.

The Anstie Grange Military Hospital

During the war ambulance trains were a common sight at Dorking's main station which was a transhipment point for stretcher cases (the incoming platform was on level ground with no steps so stretchers could be transferred easily from train to ambulance and thence on to hospitals). However, in 1916 the horrors of war were brought into the heart of the rural community.

That October Cuthbert Heath offered up his mansion near Coldharbour for use as a first-line hospital for officers. The hospital was fitted out at his own expense and run by his niece, Doreen Gore Brown. His young daughter, Genesta, acted as pantry maid. Casualties were brought directly from France via the coast and on to Holmwood station. At the station, ambulances from Aldershot would be waiting to drive the wounded to Anstie in convoy, often late at night. Stretcher-bearers gathered in front of the house half an hour before the trains were due in. Then the commandant, wearing a long white veil with a cloak and carrying a lantern, would arrive in a car to take command.

At Christmas 1916 each ward was decked with local holly and a service was conducted by Canon Chichester from St Martin's, followed by a turkey dinner and visits by the officers' families and friends. On Boxing Day the Heaths hosted the family and patients to dinner with Christmas crackers. While dinner was consumed, stockings filled with presents for each member of the household were hidden in the hall, the main staircase and corridors for patients

The Anstie Grange Military Hospital. In this photograph convalescing officers can be seen playing croquet. Anstie Grange was a twenty-six-bedroom mansion; the setting for shooting parties, hunts and balls before the war, with twenty-six indoor staff plus gardeners, stablemen and chauffeurs. After the outbreak of war the indoor staff was cut to three. (Photo courtesy of J.J. Heath-Caldwell)

Genesta Heath in 1914, aged 15. Genesta worked as a pantry maid when Anstie became a military hospital. (Image by permission of J.J. Heath-Caldwell)

The flag that flew over Anstie Grange during its time as a military hospital was later given to Genesta Heath (Hamilton) by her mother. In Kenya, where Genesta farmed after the war, it was flown on special occasions. It now hangs in Coldharbour church.

to seek out. Then bed patients were carried downstairs to watch an evening of dancing, culminating with the singing of *Auld Lang Syne* and the national anthem at 10.30pm.

In February 1917 an unexpected patient arrived on one of these convoys: Frederick Dunbar Heath, son of Cuthbert Heath's brother, Arthur Raymond Heath, and his wife Flora, who were living nearby at Kitlands. Frederick's brother had already been killed. Arthur and Flora had fallen out with Cuthbert Heath's wife, Caroline, but she lifted her prohibition on them visiting Anstie to allow them to walk over daily to see their surviving son.

Nearly 700 officers passed through the hospital, where 50 were cared for at any one time by a similar number of staff.

The certificate presented for display at Anstie Grange in 1920 in acknowledgement of the Army Council's gratitude to Cuthbert Heath. He was awarded the Order of the British Empire for his practical patriotism. The accompanying letter is signed by Winston Churchill. It hung for many years at Anstie Grange and is now on display at Dorking Museum.

CHAPTER 5

1917: Rationing, the Red Cross and the 'East End Foreigner'

By the spring of 1917 the civilian population had endured nearly three years of the deprivations of war. As the nation's resources were directed towards the production of military equipment and supply of the troops, civilians suffered shortages of food, fuel and other commodities. The shortages were exacerbated by the disruption to shipping that saw fewer imports reaching the country.

Worries about food supplies had been a feature of the war from the outset. Britain was dependent on imports; it has been estimated that 60 per cent of foodstuffs were imported in 1914. Starving Britain of food supplies was a key German tactic and submarines attacked shipping bringing supplies to the country. Shortages of imported foods had begun as early as 1915 and in 1916 the Ministry of Food was set up to ensure supplies and to prevent hoarding and profiteering by those who could afford to buy, thus depriving those who could not.

The government tried to persuade the

THINK IT OVER.

When you buy Meat from

The London Central Meat Co. Ltd.

you are not only buying the best you can possibly obtain to-day, but you are also supporting your own Colonies, and lending your influence to the maintenance of fair prices and values for the future.

Advert urging customers to buy British meat, 1917.

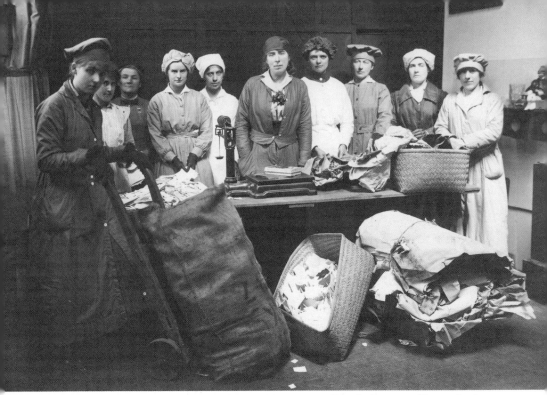

Women volunteers at Dorking's Waste Paper Supply Depot at Nower Lodge in 1917 or 1918. The women are thought to be members of the Leith Hill and District Women's Suffrage Society. Among them are Mrs Sarah Molyneux and her daughter Mary. (Photograph courtesy of John Molyneux)

nation to consume less, also to waste less. In April 1917 the Reverend Bird in Newdigate exhorted parishioners to consume less meat, bread and sugar for the sake of the war effort and to lessen the suffering of others: if the rich ate less, commodities would be less expensive for the poor. Schools provided 'war-time recipes' at children's cookery classes and speakers from the National Food Reform Association gave demonstrations on housekeeping and 'Cooking in War Time and After' in village halls, selling the demonstration foods to villagers afterwards. In March 1917 Mr and Mrs Percy Harris began one of Dorking's most successful wartime waste reduction ventures: a fund-raising waste paper depot aimed at turning waste into profit. The mostly female volunteers collected newspapers, books and magazines in village centres and sold them on to raise nearly £500 for the War Hospital Supply Depot and other charities.

Communities were also encouraged to produce more food locally. In Dorking the council procured allotment sites for the duration of the

war to enable householders to grow their own food. Potatoes were particularly scarce and the local paper warned against using seed potatoes for cooking. Older boys from the Dorking British School were tasked with cultivating the allotment plots of serving soldiers at Milton Court and Sondes Place so that production was maintained in their owners' absence. In August the council proposed a market stall for the sale of allotment produce (which was not usually permitted under allotment tenancies) in order to prevent wastage.

Dorking's pharmacist, J. Beetham Wilson, takes the opportunity to reference the fatigue of war workers in the hope of selling a tonic, 1917. When Mr Wilson was unable to import supplies of atropine for his customers in 1914 he began growing belladonna in Westcott. By 1918 the plants were ready for commercial cropping to produce the drug. In 1921 Mr Beetham Wilson chaired the town's war memorial committee.

On a larger scale, farmers were brought into the war economy. The Board of Agriculture was charged with increasing food production and given powers to determine what land should be in use and to enter onto land it deemed not being properly cultivated. In autumn 1917 the Surrey Agricultural Committee instructed the parish clerk in Newdigate to affix notices asking farmers to take active steps to destroy house sparrows that were damaging the corn crops.

Notwithstanding all these efforts, shortages continued and food prices increased. Sugar was the commodity most in demand, much of the pre-war supply having come from German and Austrian sugar beet, with the rest dependent on shipping from British colonies. The German U-boat campaign caused severe sugar shortages in 1917 and in July of that year it was rationed at 8oz a week per householder. However, having a ration card did not necessarily ensure that the householder could get hold of sugar, and grocers were able to favour some customers (who might be able to buy other foodstuffs too) over others when supplies came in.

By March 1917 it was estimated that Britain had only enough food left to last six weeks. Imported commodities had become very expensive; in particular cotton, leather and metal, as well as foodstuffs. By June food shortages were a matter of urgency. The king exhorted people to cut their bread consumption by a quarter and to use flour only for bread (rather than pastries or other items), and to refrain from feeding any grain to horses unless licensed by the Food Controller to do so where it was in the national interest. Ministers were charged with reading out this food order from pulpits throughout the land.

Difficulty in importing raw materials also directly affected the war effort. Acetone was used in the manufacture of cordite, a vital weapons propellant. Distilled from wood, before the war it was usually imported from timber-producing nations. The disruptions to shipping meant that import was no longer possible, however, and factories set to producing it from maize from the United States instead, but by 1917 the German submarine offensive threatened to cut off supplies of American maize. Upon the discovery that horse chestnuts could be used instead, the Ministry of Munitions called on children to go out and collect 'conkers' for the war effort. Though not told why the chestnuts were needed so as not to alert the Germans to the possibility of using the same method, schoolchildren spent the autumn collecting from fields and lanes. The Dorking British School alone collected 18cwts. However, it is doubtful that their conkers ever reached the factory in King's Lynn. Most of the crop rotted at railway stations because of transport difficulties, and those that did arrive turned out to be of such poor quality that production was not successful.

Food shortages and newspapers full of casualty figures took their toll on the morale of the population. School records from Holmwood,

Dorking British School May Day Festival, 1917. The celebrations feature images of the Empire and the Union flag.

DORKING MUSEUM   R269

M.O.D.—No. 253.

MONEY ORDER DEPARTMENT,
HOLLOWAY,
LONDON, N.

WAR SAVINGS CERTIFICATE.   26·9·   191 .

No. 029839.

Amount £ 19·7·6·

Purchased at Hull.

Date of Purchase 20·aug· 191 . g.y Mylae on your behalf.

The purchase of War Savings Certificate by you as shown above has been duly reported to this Department.

F. WICKHAM,

To Alice Mylae.   Controller.

NOTE.—This confirmatory notice is only sent in respect of £12 and £25 Certificates.

Alice Wylde's War Savings Certificate, 1917. War savings were introduced in 1916 to help finance the cost of the war. Individuals loaned money to the government to finance the production of war materials. Posters urged them to do so; pointing out that the soldier risked his life to win the war but that there was no risk in investing money. Investing in the war was a patriotic duty. Schools and workplaces set up war savings associations to encourage communal participation. Villages and schools set up schemes to encourage investment. The Dorking British School War Savings Association was formed in July 1916 and by the end of that year over eighty members were paying in and receiving certificates. Pressure to join the schemes could be intense. Dorking High School reported in mid-1918 that it had over sixty members after having been affiliated for four terms, subscribing £196 15s, but the term magazine editor complained vigorously of lack of response to an appeal for more members: 'Will those who have not yet joined please notice this, and see what can be done next term towards a roll of one hundred members by the end of 1918.'

Dorking and Newdigate show repeated epidemics of measles, diphtheria and whooping cough closing schools for weeks at a time. By early 1918 the numbers attending schools were at an all-time low: in Holmwood only 21 children out of 135 were in attendance on one day in January 1918, before the school closed due to a whooping cough epidemic. Teachers were also sick, and heating in the winter months was erratic. In the spring of 1917 Holmwood School had to close its

doors when it could no longer obtain coke to power the stoves. Heating for homes, offices and businesses relied on coal, and the demands of the war effort for arms manufacturing and for the steam transport that moved munitions, troops and provisions towards the Continent, meant that there was little left to supply homes. By 1915 the price of a ton of coal had reached about 40 shillings (from about 28 shillings in 1914); poorer households were finding it hard to afford coal, even when it could be obtained. Landowners such as the Duke of Norfolk began to allow selective wood-cutting on commons like Holmwood.

Manpower was also becoming critically short. In January 1917 the South Eastern Railway closed Box Hill Station (now known as Dorking Deepdene), on the east-west line, saving the employment of two staff. It did not re-open until December 1918. The great mansions surrounding Dorking suffered a huge shortage of manpower. With their large ornamental gardens, greenhouses and pleasure farms, and their multiple internal rooms, they could only be managed with multiple employees. A large estate like Denbies or Bury Hill would have had a score of people working in the house, and more in the grounds. Denbies was such a large employer before the war that it had its own church, school and volunteer fire brigade. The prolonged absence of men at war and the diversion of women into war-related work or into what had previously been 'men's work' made running mansions and grand houses impossible to pre-war standards. Rooms were closed up, exotic conservatories were neglected and lawns sown with vegetables. Some of the grand houses had been occupied or part-occupied by the military; many never returned to family use as the war exacerbated the problems of finding enough cheap labour to run them.

Deepdene had been tenanted until 1914. It was owned at the outbreak of war by the Duke of Newcastle-under-Lyme, who had inherited the mansion through his mother's family, the Hopes. The duke, however, was bankrupt and the difficulties of the war only speeded the end of Dorking's great estate. In 1917 the duke's receivers sold the great Hope art collection and other contents of the mansion at Christie's. By 1917 there was just one caretaker employed at Thomas Hope's once famous mansion.

The rich were suffering: sons and heirs were at the front, leaving sisters and elderly parents struggling to manage large houses, parks and farmland with few staff. Sometimes this could be fatal. In January

An advert for Adams store in the High Street makes reference to the war to sell its 'lighter' bags, 1917. It refers to the lack of railway porters, many of whom were serving in the forces or in work of greater importance, but with heavy leather-framed suitcases passengers still needed assistance. By 1917 one of Dorking's stations had been closed completely to save on staff.

1918 Lisma Fielding, daughter of Sir Percy and Lady Louisa of Broome Park in Betchworth, died after getting her skirt caught in the machinery of the estate's electrical generator. She had been running the estate and farm as her contribution to the war effort. Many of the absent sons and heirs would not return to rescue or inherit their mansions.

For Dorking's poorer households, death or injury at the front could be catastrophic for those left behind. The Dorking War Emergency Relief Fund saw many households unable to pay for food and fuel as a result of the death of a husband or father. In December 1916 the fund was supporting Mrs L.C. Worsfold, whose husband had been killed, while she sought a widow's pension; she was awarded 25 shillings a week. In February 1917 the fund approved a payment of 30 shillings to Mrs Stageman to allow her to visit her shellshocked son who was being treated in Warrington. When she arrived he was so distressed that he did not even recognize his mother and doctors encouraged her to

stay as long as she could as talking, they informed her, was the only means of putting him on the road to recovery. When she left she was told by the doctors that her visit had saved her boy's life. In March 1917 the fund allowed 33 shillings to the widowed Mrs Fitzgibbons to buy boots as she was finding it impossible to clothe her family of five boys on her 23 shillings a week war widow's pension. In November 1917 Mrs Hines was awarded fares of £2 to allow her and her four children to go and stay with an aunt in Bedford for sake of the family's health while her husband was in the army.

In the summer of 1917 resources came under further pressure when German Zeppelin raids struck East London. They were not the first – raids had taken place as early as January 1915 – but the raids of summer 1917 by the large Gotha GIV saw daylight attacks that caused widespread panic. The first effective raid on 13 June 1917 killed 162 people, 18 of them children (most of them under 6 years old), in Poplar, East London. Night raids commenced in September. The raids were intended to create terror and panic and to undermine morale among Londoners. Dorking was deluged with visitors terrified by the raids and seeking a safe haven in the country. Most were East End Jews. Dorking, said the local paper, had been more affected than any other country town and was becoming the home of the 'East End Foreigner'.

For a week after the first raid motor buses from Clapham to Dorking were crowded with Londoners leaving the capital. The local paper reported that Dorking had never been so full of visitors; hotels were full and apartments going at a premium. Smaller houses for rent were unobtainable. When the second wave of refugees arrived after a recurrence of air-raids they found it nearly impossible to find accommodation, mothers and children trudging the streets for hours in search of lodgings and some sleeping out in the open.

The visitors seem to have been greeted with sympathy by residents and many were found homes in the Falkland Arms district. The *Dorking and Leatherhead Advertiser* reported that some of 'the better class' had taken large furnished or unfurnished houses near the station so that they might commute to work. Those of lesser means had to settle for whatever was available and it was reported that Dorking property owners were asking high prices, fearful of the 'flitting propensities' of some 'classes of people' on the quarter day when rents were due.

The East End Jews were regarded by Dorking folk as 'foreigners'. Housing the large families was often difficult and Dorking people took some convincing that their numerous offspring were as 'quiet and orderly' and in possession of the 'juvenile virtues' of 'English' children. The 'continental customs' of the visitors also perplexed townspeople: clustering outside their doors, talking volubly, wandering in groups along the streets, and sitting in rows in the cool of the evening in open spaces.

Very soon other concerns were being raised about what the local paper termed the 'invasion'. Local traders might have benefited from the influx but others were worried by the potential lack of food as the 'invasion' exacerbated existing tensions and concerns, particularly among the less well-off, that as some foodstuffs grew scarce, the rich would not suffer scarcity. The Dorking and District branch of the National Union of Railwaymen complained to the council that their members and other workers were having difficulty obtaining sugar now that the town was being invaded by Jews:

> We ask, are these people told at the shops 'No sugar to-day'? We are inclined to think differently; as it is well known they have money to spend on other things. Further, are the upper classes given the same reply on giving their sugar order? We think not. We are repeatedly told by the shopkeepers 'no sugar to-day. We might have some to-morrow', but tomorrow never comes.

The union urged the council to ensure that outsiders did not out-buy permanent residents. In October, in an effort to dissuade people from coming down to Dorking, the council placed adverts in London newspapers saying that the town could not provide food for the influx.

The war seemed to have brought an element of radicalism to the district, perhaps inspired by the recent revolution in Russia that had been covered with grave concern by the *Dorking and Leatherhead Advertiser*. As well as suspicions that the wealthy were not suffering shortages in the same way as the rest of the population, there was a questioning among some of the pre-war status quo, and a feeling that fighting men had the right to expect better terms and conditions on their return. In December the first trade union meeting took place in the village of Newdigate, at the Village Club. Mr Banks of the National

Union of Railwaymen presided, encouraging local farm workers to organize negotiations for better wages, and to ensure that fighting men came back to better conditions than those when they left. F.E. Green, who had long written on low agricultural wages in the area, pointed out that wages in the Dorking district were lower than in Scotland where agricultural yields were far lower.

The refugee crisis also brought a large influx into overcrowded Dorking schools and Dorking British School saw its class sizes increase with children of the newcomers. The County Council issued instructions that all evacuee children should be refused admission if they remained on the books of their London schools, even if they only intended to stay temporarily. Many did return home quickly but others stayed. In December, months after the raids, Mr Hutton, the head teacher of St Paul's School, recorded the overcrowded conditions in the lower part of his school 'owing to the number of children who are temporarily staying in Dorking'. It was not until February 1919 that the last of the London raid refugees returned to their homes.

In the meantime the council considered the possibility of devastation from the air, proposing the use of the town's caves as air-raid shelters should the need arise.

On 2 April 1917 the United States entered the war as a result of unrestricted German submarine activity and the consequent sinking of American merchant shipping. Although American troops did not see action until the following year, the entry of the United States into the war gave the British nation a boost and hope. However, in the shorter term the Western Front remained pretty impregnable to assaults by the British and French.

Some could not see the point in fighting it out to the bitter end. Mr Pethick-Lawrence of The Mascot in Holmwood announced that he was to stand as the 'Peace by Negotiation' candidate in the by-election in South Aberdeen. The concept of a negotiated peace settlement was promoted by peace campaigners across the nation, but it had little popular support and Mr Pethick-Lawrence was not successful.

With appreciation of the vital part that the Red Cross was playing in the war, Red Cross Week in June of 1917 was a huge affair in Dorking and the villages. Running from 13 to 23 June, it raised over £6,000 for the British Red Cross Society, the British Farming Red Cross Fund and the Dorking War Hospital Supply Depot. It was the

biggest event of the war years. The programme included a baby show, parades, whist drives, concerts, an operetta in the Public Halls, an auction of donated items, an agricultural sale, a flag day, a concert by the English Folk Song Quartet, a bowling tournament and a gutter sale. At the procession on 20 June the Dorking British School's decorated car, symbolizing Britannia, her colonies and dependencies, took first prize.

The highlight was the grand garden fête in the grounds of Pippbrook on Wednesday 20 June. The fête featured the band of the 48th Highlanders of Canada and the town band, a floral procession, maypole dances from villagers, performances by local schools, Morris dancing from local groups, potato shies (in the absence of coconuts), a shooting gallery, a 'melting pot' for unwanted jewellery, and a 'war cakes' stand. The Dorking British School presented a series of tableaux on the history of the conflict, illustrating 'the present unequalled struggle and sacrifice of right and might'. Key scenes in the history of the conflict, from the threat to Serbia in 1914, culminated in a rendition of the *Battle Song of the Republic*, followed by *God Save the King*. The tableaux were so popular that they were presented again on 28 June.

At the public auction of donated items large amounts of silver, pictures, china, furniture and wine were donated from Abinger, Betchworth, Brockham, Capel and Beare Green, Coldharbour, Dorking, Holmwood, Holmbury St Mary, Leigh, Mickleham, Newdigate, Westcott and Wotton. The 1,500 lots raised £1,688. The Agricultural Gift Sale of 21 June was a day of jollity. It began with an auction of a Gallipoli oak, brought back by an officer of the Surrey Yeomanry. One of the principal entertainments was the auctioning of the '£1000 donkey' presented by the Right Honourable the Lord Northbrook. It had been sold the previous year in Guildford to raise funds for the Relief of the Allies Fund, where it raised £188. By the time it reached Dorking it had been repeatedly auctioned to raise money for charitable causes. Before it was auctioned in Dorking, Lady Lawrence of Burford Lodge was dared to ride the animal through the market with £1 (a significant sum at the time) to be donated to the fund if she did so. Lady Lawrence took the bet. Great amusement was caused when traffic through the town was held up by her progress and the fund-raising committee went along stranded cars and buses extracting donations from their drivers and occupants. More money

Dorking and District Red Cross Week.

In aid of
The British Red Cross Society, The British Farmers' Red Cross Fund, The Dorking War Hospital Supply Depot.

Chairman: Major H. H. GORDON CLARK, D.L., J.P.
Vice-Chairman: JAMES A. WHITE, Esq., J.P.
Hon. Treasurers: F. PERCY HARRIS, Esq., and THE MANAGERS OF THE LOCAL BANKS.
Joint Hon. Secretaries: LEWIS CROW and ARTHUR H. LYNE.

PROGRAMME

... of the ...

Grand Garden Fete

to be held in the Grounds of

PIPPBROOK HOUSE, DORKING

(By kind permission of H. GURNEY AGGS, Esq.).

On Wednesday, June 20th, 1917.

To be formally opened at 2.15 p.m. by

Col. Sir JOHN NORTON GRIFFITHS, K.C.B., M.P., D.S.O.

GATES OPEN AT 1.30 P.M.

Admission 1/-; after 4 p.m., 6d. *Wounded Soldiers admitted Free.*

HEAD OFFICE: 12 HIGH STREET, DORKING.

DORKING AND DISTRICT

RED CROSS WEEK.

In aid of the British Red Cross Society, the British Farmers' Red Cross Fund, and the Dorking War Hospital Supply Depot.

Programme of Events.

WEDNESDAY, JUNE 13th. DORKING LOCAL BABY SHOW. DANCE at the Oddfellows' Hall (Tickets 2/-) Arranged by Mr. SLEIGH.

FRIDAY, JUNE 15th. Private View of Entries for Sale at the Public Hall, Dorking. Admission 6d.

SATURDAY, JUNE 16th. Public View of Entries for Sale. Admission by Catalogue, price 1/-

SUNDAY, JUNE 17th. SPECIAL COLLECTION IN PLACES OF WORSHIP.
CHURCH PARADE OF VOLUNTEERS at St. Martin's, Dorking.

MONDAY, JUNE 18th. SALE OF FURNITURE, JEWELLERY, &c., at the Public Hall, Dorking.
WHIST DRIVE at the Betchworth Park Golf Club (or if wet at the Drill Hall, Dorking).

TUESDAY, JUNE 19th. SALE OF FURNITURE, JEWELLERY, &c., continued.
POPULAR CONCERT at Oddfellows' Hall, at 8 p.m.

WEDNESDAY, JUNE 20th. GARDEN FETE in the Grounds of Pippbrook House, Dorking, kindly lent by Mr. H. GURNEY AGGS. Maypole and Morris Dancing. Floral Procession. Stalls for the Sale of all sorts of Articles. Bands of the 48th Highlanders of Canada and the Dorking Town Band. Championship Baby Show. Shooting Gallery. Refreshments. Entertainments. Dancing and all kinds of Amusements.

THURSDAY, JUNE 21st. AGRICULTURAL SALE in the Market Place, Dorking, to be opened by COL. R. H. RAWSON, M.P. Flag Day throughout the district. Operetta at the Public Hall, Dorking, organised by Mr. COUSIN, entitled "Britannia, the Queen of the Ocean."

FRIDAY, JUNE 22nd. VOCAL CONCERT at the Public Hall, Dorking, at 5 p.m., by the English Folk Song Quartette.

SATURDAY, JUNE 23rd. BOWLING TOURNAMENT on the Dorking Bowling Green, West Street. TEAS.
GUTTER MARKET SALE in Evening (7 p.m.)

The Competitions will be drawn by Mr. Pardon-Howe, Esq., J.P., C.C., from the steps of the Red Lion Hotel, at 7 p.m.

Concerts, Whist Drives or Entertainments in the Villages
IN AID OF THE FUND,

Head Office: 12, HIGH STREET, DORKING.

Programme of events for Dorking Red Cross Week 1917 and programme for the garden fête.

DORKING AND DISTRICT

WEEK.

CATALOGUE

OF THE

GREAT GIFT SALE

AT THE

PUBLIC HALL, DORKING.

Monday and Tuesday, June 18th & 19th, 1917.

Sale to commence at 11 a.m.

Price 1s.

ROWE'S Printing Works, Dorking.

Dorking Red Cross Week sale catalogue, June 1917. The catalogue lists the jewellery and goods donated according to donor and village.

The BAND of the

48th Highlanders of Canada

will play:

March	"Black Watch"
Selection	"Melody Land"
Waltz	"Girl on the Film"
Cornet Solo	"In the Shadow of your Eyes"
Intermezzo	"Stepping Stones"
Patrol	"Canadian Patrol"
March ...	"Highlanders! Fix Bayonets"

"GOD SAVE THE KING."

Bandmaster: R. LODGE,
134th Battalion C.E.F. (48th Highlanders).

The Dorking Town Band

will play Selections throughout the Afternoon and Evening.

Programme of Tableaux.

Arranged by Mr. S. COUSIN.

At 5 and 7 p.m. *Admission 6d.*

Illustrating the present unequalled struggle and sacrifice of Right and Might.

1. Conspiracy.
2. "Necessity knows no law."
3. To the Rescue.
4. Help from over the Sea.
5. Treachery.
6. Treachery held in check.
7. Desperation.
8. Enter U.S.A.
9. "Shall we?" "If so,—when?"

Battle Song of the American Republic.

God Save the King.

Programme for the garden fête held at Pippbrook on 20 June 1917 for Dorking Red Cross Week. Patriotic tableaux on war-related subjects, culminating in the entry of the Americans into the war, featured among the entertainments. In 1917 the house was owned by Mrs Gurney Aggs; it has since seen use as council offices and the town library.

Catalogue for the Agricultural Sale held as part of Dorking's Red Cross Week in 1917. The first items for auction were the donkey donated by Lord Northbrook, followed by a Gallipoli oak brought back by a local member of the Surrey Yeomanry, bringing an element of topicality to the proceedings.

Children of the Dorking British School in costume for their cantata of Britannia performed at Red Cross Week in June 1917.

Lady Lawrence of Burford Lodge during her 'dare' to ride the £1,000 donkey through Dorking High Street to raise funds for the Red Cross in June 1917.

was made by charging for donkey rides. Bidding for the donkey started at £1 and it was finally won by Mrs Greville of Polesden Lacey for £25. Her representative immediately passed it on to the Farmers' Red Cross Fund for re-auction. Afterwards a picture of Lady Lawrence on the donkey was auctioned and two German flags were sold at the 'Gutter Market' and burned in the High Street.

All the villages held their own events. The *Dorking Advertiser* commented on the fête at Newdigate Place that the village presented a merry scene. Its summing-up of that event could well have been applied to the whole week, or even the year: 'the long absence of pleasure had made everyone determined to enjoy themselves.'

Two Christmas cards from the album of Dora Livermore, who was working as a nurse in France.

This year I've guns and carriages,
And military marriages;
Plum puddings, lots of baccy,
For warriors clad in Khaki;
Some push for the boys that are brave,
And some ships for the ocean wave.
I've lots of Camaraderie,
And the certain hope of VICTORY!

I'm sad for the boys that are gone,
But I say, none the less, "CARRY ON!"
Carry on against odds that are mighty
For the sake of dear old BLIGHTY.
Brave hearts, I cry, Better Cheer,
Please God, I'll bring PEACE NEXT YEAR.

The Diary of Kenneth Harman Young

Kenneth Harman Young kept a diary of his wartime experiences. Born in 1887 in Dorking, he attended Charterhouse School and in February 1906 he was articled to train as a solicitor at Withers. His brother Henry was killed in 1915 and Kenneth failed two medicals before finally being accepted to enlist in November 1916 in the 15th London Regiment (The Prince of Wales' Own Civil Service Rifles). Wounded twice and with severe shellshock, he was advised to pursue an outdoor life. After the war he studied agriculture and rented Upper House Farm from his father in Ewhurst. His diary, which records his time in the trenches, was shipped back to England when he was injured and rescued from a torpedoed ship.

Kenneth Harman Young.

The Pethick-Lawrences: Pacifists in the 'War to end all wars'

Until a disagreement with the Pankhursts in 1912, the social campaigner Emmeline Pethick-Lawrence (1867–1954) had been treasurer of the Women's Social and Political Union, the leading militant organization in the fight for the vote for women in Britain. A popular speaker, she had raised large sums of money, been to prison six times, and founded and edited *Votes for Women* with her husband Frederick. He had given legal advice to the movement and personally stood bail for 1,000 women.

The couple lived at The Mascot (now known as The Dutch House) in South Holmwood, which was where they heard of the assassination of Archduke Franz Ferdinand in the summer of 1914. The outbreak of war wrought a split within the suffrage movement. Mrs Pankhurst and her daughter, Christabel, called a halt to campaigning and set to recruiting, in the hope of winning respect for women's contribution to the war effort. However, for Emmeline Pethick-Lawrence, as for the more socially radical Sylvia Pankhurst,

the cause of international peace was a natural extension of her fight for women's rights and the outbreak of war a confirmation of her belief that leaving political power solely in the hands of men was unwise. Both Emmeline and Fred, and many others disappointed by the Pankhursts' stance, continued to campaign for women's suffrage, albeit in a more low-key way, throughout the war, but turned much of their energies to campaigning for peace.

In 1914 Emmeline brought Belgian refugees to Holmwood through the Women's Emergency Corps, attempting to do what she could for the cause of humanity rather than nation. She was invited to speak to women's groups in the then neutral United States and in November 1914 she told an audience in New York that the campaign for the vote must go on. She did not think that the war would not have happened if women had the vote, but she did think that women's influence could work to prevent war in general. This message found a sympathetic audience among New York women not keen to become embroiled in a European war.

The Sundial, a few hundred metres north of the Pethick-Lawrences' home in South Holmwood, was built by the couple in 1904 as a holiday home for disadvantaged London mothers and their children. It housed Belgian refugees in 1914.

In April 1915 she attended the International Women's Congress for Peace at The Hague. She was one of only three British delegates to attend, having travelled directly to The Hague from the United

States with the American delegation; the British government prevented all but two others from attending by withdrawing passports and suspending the ferry service to Dutch ports. On her return Emmeline campaigned for a mediated settlement and against conscription, becoming treasurer of the Women's International League of Great Britain (affiliated with the International Committee of Women for Permanent Peace, now the Women's International League for Peace and Freedom).

Emmeline Pethick-Lawrence (far left) with international delegates aboard the liner Noordam on their way to The Hague Peace Conference in April 1915. (Photograph courtesy of the Library of Congress)

The Mascot became a weekend retreat for Emmeline's war-haunted London circle: her brother, Harold, returned from Canada to enlist, leaving his wife Evie in Holmwood. Her sister, Dr Marie Pethick, took refuge there from the stresses of repeated night calls to air-raid casualties; Emmeline was devastated when Marie collapsed and died suddenly while taking casualties to the Euston Road Women's Hospital. Emmeline's own London apartment at Clement's Inn on The Strand suffered war damage, forcing the couple to abandon their London home.

Emmeline continued to lobby for the vote through a campaigning organization named the United Suffragists throughout the war. Had

women like her not kept the issue in the mind of politicians, it is unlikely that women would have achieved even the limited franchise that they did in 1918. In 1918 Emmeline stood as the Labour candidate for Rusholme in Manchester, advocating a just settlement with Germany as a necessity for the achievement of permanent peace. She was not elected.

COMING EVENTS

The United Suffragists will hold a public meeting in the small Portman Rooms, Baker Street, W., on Thursday, July 15, from 3 to 5 p.m. Speaker: Mrs. Pethick Lawrence. Chair: Mr. John Scurr. Admission free.

Notice of a meeting of the United Suffragists with Emmeline as a speaker, July 1916. Unlike Emmeline and Christabel Pankhurst who gave up campaigning for the vote for the duration of the war, Emmeline Pethick-Lawrence and the United Suffragists continued to campaign for the vote and their magazine Votes for Women dealt extensively with women's issues arising from the war.

Emmeline's husband, Frederick Pethick-Lawrence (1871–1961), was treasurer of the Union of Democratic Control, the leading anti-war movement to which many left-leaning politicians, journalists and intellectuals became affiliated. In 1917 he stood as the 'Peace by Negotiation' candidate in the South Aberdeen by-election. He lost.

In 1918 Fred was conscripted, at the age of 46. He refused to serve on the grounds that he was an objector, albeit of a political rather than a conscientious kind, favouring a negotiated peace rather than a fight until unconditional surrender. His case came before the Dorking Military Tribunal, one of whose members, Alfred Keep of Holmwood, was a key member of the Dorking branch of the League for Opposing Women's Suffrage. Fred was awarded an exemption as long as he did work of 'national importance'. He was offered labouring work at 35 shillings a week by Frederick Ernest Green at his smallholding at Cudworth near Newdigate.

Green was an old comrade who had written for the *Votes for Women* publication. He had acquired a number of plots of land from the socialist Smallholdings Association that had bought several hundred acres in Cudworth before the war to provide small-scale farming opportunities. Though not affiliated to any political party, Green had made a name for himself as a writer on social and labour issues relating to agriculture. At Cudworth he had built a modern cottage, Baringsfield, from which he extolled the virtues of country life and dispensed advice on bee-keeping, soft fruits and poultry-keeping to would-be homesteaders from the city whose children, he wrote, in *The Awakening of England*, would 'live intimately with the winds, the clouds and Mother Earth'. Green campaigned against child labour and low agricultural wages throughout the war. His son, David, was reported killed in 1917, only to resurface with a Military Cross the following year. Cudworth was something of a magnet for socialist utopian experiments: socialist John Aitcheson had set up summer camps there that were used by Labour youth organizations. Aitcheson was also awarded exemption from service on account of his views.

Whether the Military Tribunal did not like these suffragettes and socialists looking after their own or whether the work really was not of significance, we do not know, but the tribunal rejected Green's proposal and Fred Pethick-Lawrence was dispatched instead to labour at Wattlehurst Farm in Capel at 27 shillings a week. An application for exemption on behalf of the Pethick-Lawrences' faithful driver, who had ferried all the luminaries of the pre-war suffrage campaigns and was now working as their gardener, was refused.

In the euphoria of victory it was clear that as an anti-war candidate who had favoured a negotiated settlement and had not fought, Fred stood no chance of winning a parliamentary seat in the 1918 election. He withdrew his candidacy for the Labour party in Hastings. Deploring the Versailles settlement, he predicted another war.

He was finally elected to Parliament in 1923 and went on to become Clement Attlee's Secretary of State for India in the Labour government of 1945. A long-time supporter of Indian independence, he had discussed passive resistance with Gandhi, who visited him

in Peaslake in 1933. As Secretary of State for India he had the pleasure of negotiating Indian independence in 1946/7. He ended his life as 1st Baron Lawrence of Peaslake, to where the couple moved in 1920.

When the Pethick-Lawrences left Holmwood in 1920 they sold The Sundial to one of their pacifist circle who had also been an objector during the war, the journalist John Langdon-Davies (1897–1941). He went on to found the charity PLAN during the Spanish Civil War. He is pictured here in later life with his two small sons.

CHAPTER 6

1918: Armistice

By the beginning of 1918 the public was war-weary. New Year messages from parish magazines talked only of trials to come, and of all doing their bit to shorten the war. 'Let us do our best,' asked the Reverend Bird from Newdigate, 'and have our consciences clear.' In particular they talked about food.

Rationing of food started at the beginning of 1918, firstly with sugar. The British tactic of attempting to blockade German supplies had resulted in the German response of total U-boat (submarine) warfare, disrupting imports of food to Britain from around the world. Rationing was intended to ensure fairer distribution of food, and thereby stop long food queues (which meant time wasted and lost to the war effort). Ration cards entitled people to a weekly ration of meat and butter or margarine. Although rationing and an orderly distribution of food did away with food queues, many working people could not afford to buy what was on the meat ration. In March the *Dorking and Leatherhead Advertiser* called for edible offal and bones to be sold without coupons to alleviate the hardship of poorer families.

On 21 March Germany launched a major offensive on the Western Front, only its second of the war. Dorking lost another eleven men in what became known as the Kaiser's Offensive, a last-ditch attempt to push through to a decisive position before the arrival of American troops. The Germans achieved their biggest successes since 1915, claiming back swathes of territory so expensively gained by the British and French over the previous year and taking large numbers of prisoners, but ultimately the British and French line held. It was to be

Germany's last real push forward of the war. With the Americans on the way and the great offensive held off, there were signs of confidence in parish magazines by mid-April. By June 1918 2 million American troops were on their way to France: they first faced fire on the night of 8/9 June and the Germans launched their last offensive on 15 July in the Champagne-Marne area where they were repulsed by the rejuvenated French. German troops were exhausted, their food supplies were low and revolution was threatened in Berlin. However, the war was not yet over.

The British army was seriously short of troops and men had to be released from munitions work and from the mines to swell the ranks. The recruitment age was raised to 50. In the last months of the war, many men who had been exempt from military service because they worked on the land were finally conscripted. In June the Dorking Military Tribunal was instructed that no fit man of fighting age should receive exemption on occupational grounds unless he was engaged in work directly important to the preparation of war. In August Walter Dudley, a 46-year-old poultry farmer from Cudworth, managed to obtain a two-month exemption on the basis of having 500 birds under

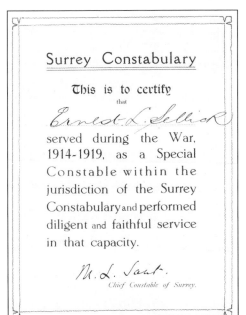

Surrey Constabulary

This is to certify

that

Ernest L. Sellick

served during the War, 1914-1919, as a Special Constable within the jurisdiction of the Surrey Constabulary and performed diligent and faithful service in that capacity.

M. L. Sant.

Chief Constable of Surrey.

Ernest Sellick's certificate for serving as a special constable. Because of his importance as an experienced solicitor's clerk, Mr Sellick remained exempt from serving in the armed forces despite the shortages of men in the war's last months.

his care that had produced 20,000 eggs since the previous October. He was planning to double his stock, marketing cockerels as soon as they were ready and bringing £700 to £800 worth of chicken meat to market. Yet even he was not given a full long-term exemption.

Increased manpower in France meant acute shortages at home, the prospect of not being able to bring in harvests, and the spectre of mass hunger. Calls were made on older schoolchildren to work on the land. In the spring of 1918 the headmaster of Dorking High School called for volunteers to form an agricultural working party for the summer and a squad of twenty boys was sent off to work on farms in Devizes in Wiltshire. The editor of the school report claimed that they were looking forward to being of some use as well as to having a pleasant time: 'For most of us it will be the first experience of camp life, but we hope not the last. No doubt we shall have some yarns to spin.'

Foraging and fruit-gathering that had been done on an ad hoc basis was now organized. In September 1918 children took part in a nationwide blackberrying initiative, run by the National Preservation of Food Scheme. Children scoured the countryside for edible fruit that was taken to the food control office in Dorking and then forwarded to London. School heads regarded such initiatives with mixed feelings, as if children were allowed out foraging they would not get an attendance mark at school and attendances were recorded for funding purposes. So schools, facing a loss of income, were often reluctant to allow children to participate. Eventually Surrey Education Committee allowed children taken out for blackberry-picking expeditions to receive their attendance mark. In 1918 Newdigate School, which had previously closed on two afternoons a week for the blackberry season, stayed open, taking thirty-five children out to pick. St Paul's School sent groups of girls and boys up to Ranmore. In 1918 the boys collected 92lb (42kg) of fruit and the girls 193lb (88kg).

In April women who had earned an armlet for working more than 30 days (or 240 hours) on the land were invited by the Dorking District Committee of the Women's Branch of the Board of Agriculture to tea at St Martin's Church room. Afterwards they were presented with stripes in recognition of their work at the Public Halls. The Land Army had been formed the previous year and Prime Minister David Lloyd George called for women to join. After training, women were issued with a masculine uniform of breeches and boots and a green armband

COMPANY-SERGEANT-MAJOR.

To all the slackers on parade, to all those who are " green,"
To those who've never been before, although they should have been,
To A and B and C and D and several others like them,
To those who always act the fool when anybody passes,
To " What's his name" and " You know who," to all of them I cry :
" Just pull yourselves together, for the General's coming by."

To all who think they're funny when their hats are on the slant,
To those who given orders, mutter sulkily. " I sha'n't,"
To any hopeless lout who scrapes his feet at every chance,
To those who slouch, and " Spring-heeled Jacks " who walk with
     sprightly prance,
To " What's his name," and " You know who," to each of them I sigh :
" Oh, pull yourselves together, there's a Colonel coming by."

When A and B and C and D have head and shoulders back,
When all are marching steadily with rifle and with pack,
When feet don't drag like leaden weights, and arms are freely swinging,
When step is kept in perfect time by *everybody* singing,
To A, and B, and C, and D, to everyone I cry :
" Now keep yourselves together though there's no one coming by.

                                                              Pip.

A poem appearing in the Dorking High School termly magazine, summer term 1918.

with a red crown. In October the *Dorking and Leatherhead Advertiser* reported that demand for Land Army women far exceeded supply as farmers tried to bring in harvests with little labour, and that farmers employing the women were 'practically unanimous in their praises'.

Supplies of munitions also had to be kept up. Sales of National War Bonds and War Savings Certificates had fallen locally – perhaps out of complacency that the war would soon be over – and a national effort was made to encourage investment. Dorking also held a War Weapons Week from 8 to 13 July.

The allied Hundred Days' Offensive began in August 1918 with the Battle of Amiens which blasted a 15-mile gap in the German lines, allowing an advance of 14 miles. The following Battle of Albert put unrelenting pressure on the Germans, who retreated to the Hindenburg Line in the south. September saw the allies advance to the Hindenburg Line in the north and centre. German generals realized that the war could not be won, but the Kaiser fought on in the hope of retaining a negotiating position and of concluding separate peace treaties with the allied nations rather than accepting outright defeat.

With victory looking likely, thoughts turned to memorials for the dead. In Holmwood Arthur Bryans and his wife Annie of Holmwood

Cottage installed a triptych window to sit over the altar. It was dedicated in expectation of the end of the war. 'Can it be possible,' asked the *Dorking and Leatherhead Advertiser* in early October, 'that now we may hear the fluttering of the wings of the peace-angel, and that this Advent season will prove of a surety that the spirit of the Child is mightier than big battalions, and that ideas are stronger than strategists?' The hand of God was certainly seen in the defeat of Germany.

Finally, on 11 November 1918 the war ended. With millions of American soldiers arriving, the allies pushed back the demoralized German defence through France. Germany's allies fell away as defeat became inevitable, the German navy mutinied against what they saw as a suicidal defence, and revolution was threatened at home. When President Wilson of the United States demanded the abdication of the Kaiser as a condition of peace, Germany declared itself a republic.

Dorking received the news with much rejoicing, though 'subdued and restrained in the consciousness of all the sorrow the war has entailed', wrote the local paper. Mr E.W. Attlee of the town mill and feed stores received an official message in the early evening and at six o'clock the anti-aircraft gun heralded the news. Flags and other bunting appeared in all directions, expressing victory in international code. 'Peace by Victory' was suspended across the High Street from Mr Beetham-Wilson's pharmacy. The town band played patriotic airs outside the Red Lion Hotel to a large audience, the streets were filled with rejoicing people, and in the waning light fireworks spluttered and banged. The telephone rang all day at Anstie Grange Military Hospital at Coldharbour and a dance was hastily arranged (although there was only one man available with whom to dance). In Newdigate the children attended special war lessons, saluted the flag and sang patriotic songs.

THE SIGNING OF PEACE.

HOW DORKING RECEIVED THE NEWS.

Dorking received the good news of the signing of the Peace Treaty with much rejoicing, though subdued and re-trained in the consciousness of all the sorrow the war has entailed. Mr. E. W. Attlee received an official message in the early evening in his capacity as chief citizen of the town, and at six o'clock the anti-aircraft gun heralded the news further abroad. At once flags and other bunting appeared in all directions, conspicuous being the International Naval Code, "Peace by Victory," suspended across the High-street, from the premises of Mr. J. B. Wilson, to the London Boot Stores. The Town Band, conducted by Mr. Snelling, played patriotic airs outside the Red Lion Hotel, and had a large audience. In fact, the streets were filled by a rejoicing people, and in the waning light fireworks spluttered and banged.

BONFIRE IN HIGH STREET.

The more rollicking spirits appeared to have reserved some of their enthusiasm for Monday evening, and when all good people should have been in bed, they were playing high jinks in the centre of the High-street. Rockets ascended skywards, the darkness was illuminated by coloured lights, and an impromptu bonfire in the centre of the street, near the White Horse Hotel, proved a fitting finale. Fuel mysteriously appeared from all directions, and to the refrain, "Keep the home fires burning," the flames were fed till well past midnight.

THANKSGIVING SERVICES.

In a spirit of thanksgiving vast numbers of people throughout the land flocked to the churches on the first Peace Sunday for close on five years.

Dorking and Leatherhead Advertiser article 'How Dorking received the news' of the Armistice.

The following day children were given a half-day off school to celebrate. The paper commented that 'the more rollicking spirits had enthusiasm for Monday evening and playing high jinks in the High Street.' Rockets and fireworks were set off and an impromptu bonfire in the centre of the High Street near the White Horse saw people singing *Keep the Home Fires Burning* as they brought wood. The flames were kept alight until after midnight. On the first Sunday after the Armistice people flocked to local churches as vicars gave thanks and played the national anthem.

A mug produced to celebrate the Armistice in Dorking. The reverse side depicts the Dorking cockerel. (Photo reproduced with permission of Roy Williamson)

'How long we have lived in these four years,' wrote the editor of the *Dorking and Leatherhead Advertiser*. 'So long in their intensity that it is only when we are able for a moment to put away the present and recall the old questions that stirred us in peace times, the old pleasures and hopes and grumblings, that we realise how altered everything is. This war has absorbed our energies and centred our

thoughts. Even to talk of anything else has bored us. We have breathed it as an atmosphere, worked for it as a life purpose, sacrificed for it as a religion, and if called to give our best love have felt as if we were giving them to God. It has been unlike all other wars in the world's history.'

During the Second World War the town of Dorking adopted HMS Titania *during Warship Week in 1942. HMS* Titania *had already seen service in 1914–18. She was purchased while under construction as a merchant ship at the Clyde Shipbuilding Company yard in Glasgow for conversion to a submarine depot ship in 1915. In 1916 she headed up the 11th Submarine Flotilla. At the end of the Great War she was sent to Hong Kong, where she remained until 1939. (Photo reproduced with permission of Roy Williamson)*

Bertha Broadwood of Lyne House in Capel, anti women's suffrage campaigner and founder of the Holt-Ockley village nursing organization, wrote one of her poems for the occasion:

Whom have we British fought? The Devil incarnate.
First temper, then forceful driver of a slave,–
A would-be tyrant over kingdoms, Church and state,–
A maniac: manacled 'gainst mercy's sign to save!
How have we fought? – Beside our foes of but ten decades past,
Starting mere thousands! Despised of many-millioned enemy
Who dreamt of crushing Britain's power, then France at last –
After some forty years of 'peaceful' pushing treachery –
with all his devil-master's will to spoil and damn,
Through abuse of Heaven – born laws of science and of art,
Regardless of honour's faith towards God, or man,
Fiendishly confident to cowe, or kill man, body, soul and heart.
And God our hope, wearied by braggart's blasphemies
Has justified His word, as each free nation now rejoicing sees.

There is no sign in Bertha's tortuous verse of any appreciation of the changes that the war had brought, or anticipation of the changed circumstances that its aftermath would bring to the post-war world; neither in its poetry and imagery, nor in its social structures and political allegiances. As far as Bertha and many others were concerned, it was 'job done' and back to normal.

Christmas card from the album of Dora Livermore, 1918. Dora was still in France after the Armistice, working with German prisoners of war.

Growing Belladonna

One commodity that was being grown in quantity was belladonna (otherwise known as deadly nightshade). The plant is used to produce the drug atropine, which has a myriad of medical uses. Before the war all supplies in use in Britain came from Germany. When that supply became unavailable in 1914, Dorking chemist Mr J. Beetham-Wilson started growing it on three plots in Westcott. The plants must be four years old before they are commercially profitable and in May 1918 it was announced that the plant was being harvested in Dorking on a scale large enough to preclude shortages in the future and that doctors would be able to prescribe it again.

Charles Robertson VC

In April 1918 Lance Corporal Charles Graham Robertson of the 10th Battalion the Royal Fusiliers was awarded Great Britain's highest military honour, the Victoria Cross. The award was made in recognition of acts of bravery performed near Ypres.

Lance Corporal Charles Robertson VC.

Charles Robertson (1879–1954) was born in Yorkshire but came to Dorking as a boy when his father was employed as a gardener at Riverdale in Pixham. After attending St Martin's and Dorking High schools, he joined the army. He served in the Boer War but came to regard that war as dishonourable and preferred not to talk about his part in it. On his return from service he became a railway booking clerk in Dorking. He also played football for Dorking and was a keen member of the Old Dorking Swimming Club that raced in the river at Castle Mill.

Robertson was recalled to service when the First World War broke out. In early 1918 he found himself in the thick of the fighting to stem the German advance near Ypres after the March breakthrough known as the Kaiser's Offensive. Further progress would have seen the Germans reach the Channel ports, with

disastrous consequences. Robertson repelled a strong German attack on his position. Realizing he was about to be cut off, he sent two men for reinforcements while he and another held the position, firing his Lewis gun at the advancing Germans. No reinforcements arrived but Robertson continued to hold the position, firing alone when his companion was killed. Twice he had to move further back but he continued to fight, though wounded and under heavy machine-gun fire, until his ammunition was exhausted. Without his actions the Germans would have been able to make a much swifter advance in his sector.

Lance Corporal Robertson VC in military uniform as featured in the Dorking and Leatherhead Advertiser, 1918.

Wounded in the stomach, Robertson was not expected to survive. However, after being evacuated to England and undergoing intricate surgery, he made an unexpected recovery. On 5 April the *London Gazette* announced that he had been awarded the Victoria Cross. On 20 April the *Dorking and Leatherhead Advertiser* reported him writing from his hospital bed that it was 'the biggest shock of my life'. 'My word,' he wrote, 'I shall be suffering from a swelled head.'

'There is a strong desire that some public recognition should be made,' said the paper, claiming that the honour was reflected on his native town. 'It is not given to every town to possess its VC.'

Dorking Urban District Council undertook a public collection to raise funds so that the town might honour him, but Robertson rejected any 'fuss'. He agreed to accept a gold watch and chain but asked that any other monies raised be put to charitable use. In December 1918, after his presentation with the medal at Buckingham Palace, thousands turned out to see Lance Corporal Robertson presented with his watch. He was brought by horse-drawn carriage to the High Street in procession with Boy Scouts, Girl Guides, schoolchildren and the town band. At the High Street the horses were unharnessed and the carriage was drawn to the Red Lion Inn by Silver Badge soldiers (who had been discharged from service

Numb. 30619.

DORKING MUSEUM

4297

SIXTH SUPPLEMENT

TO

The London Gazette.

Of FRIDAY, the 5th of APRIL, 1918.

Published by Authority.

The Gazette is registered at the General Post Office for transmission by Inland Post as a newspaper. The postage rate to places within the United Kingdom, for each copy, is one halfpenny for the first 6 ozs., and an additional halfpenny for each subsequent 6 ozs. or part thereof. For places abroad the rate is a halfpenny for every 2 ounces, except in the case of Canada, to which the Canadian Magazine Postage rate applies.

TUESDAY, 9 APRIL, 1918.

War Office,
9th April, 1918.

His Majesty the KING has been graciously pleased to approve of the award of the Victoria Cross to the undermentioned Non-Commissioned Officer :—

No. G.58769 L./Cpl. Charles Graham Robertson, M.M., R. Fus. (Merstham).

For most conspicuous gallantry and devotion to duty in repelling a strong attack by the enemy on our position. On realising that he was being cut off, L./Cpl. Robertson sent back two men to get reinforcements, and remained at his post (with only one other man), firing his Lewis gun and killing large numbers of the enemy, who were in range on his right. No reinforcements came up, and, realising that he was being completely cut off, he withdrew with the only other survivor of the garrison of the post, to a point about ten yards further back where he successfully held his position.

Here he again stayed for some considerable time, firing his Lewis gun and inflicting casualties on the enemy. The position was, however, made impossible for him by the heavy hostile bombing and machine-gun fire, so he was forced to again withdraw, and arrived at a defended post. At this post he got on top of the parapet with a comrade, mounted his gun in a shell-hole, and continued firing at the enemy, who were pouring across the top of and down an adjacent trench. He had not been firing long when his comrade was killed, and he himself severely wounded. He managed to crawl back, bringing his gun with him, but could no longer fire it, as he had exhausted all his ammunition.

L./Cpl. Robertson was alone throughout these operations, except for the presence of one other man who later was killed, and the most determined resistance and fine fight which he put up undoubtedly prevented the enemy from making a more rapid advance. His initiative and resource, and the magnificent fighting spirit, are worthy of the highest praise.

Victoria Cross citation from the London Gazette, 5 April 1918.

Lance Corporal Robertson with town dignitaries on the day of his procession through Dorking.

through injury). At the Red Lion, which was decorated in red, white and blue, Lord Ashcombe and the local MP made speeches and Robertson was presented with his watch.

After the war Robertson returned to the railway, commuting from Longfield Road to the LNER's London offices. According to his obituary he was happiest when watching cricket or football, playing a game of snooker or walking on Box Hill. He also played an active part in town institutions. During the Second World War he was a sergeant in the Home Guard. Lance Corporal Robertson is buried in Dorking Cemetery.

Miss Daisy Wadling's Military Funeral

In September 1918 Daisy Wadling, daughter of Lieutenant Colonel Wadling of Townfield, received a full military funeral at Dorking Cemetery.

Daisy Wadling was serving as a driver in the Army Service Corps when she caught a cold while driving to Chatham on duty. The 'cold' turned out to be influenza and Daisy succumbed to pneumonia after having been transferred to the Endell Street Military Hospital in London's Covent Garden. The hospital was run by a staff of women doctors, mainly ex-suffragette campaigners, under Dr Flora Murray and Dr Louisa (daughter of Britain's first woman doctor, Elizabeth) Garrett Anderson.

The women had established a hospital in France at the beginning of the war (unable to do so in Britain since they had all gained criminal records for their part in suffragette campaigns). Transferring to London, Murray and Anderson sought to prove to the authorities that women were capable of establishing and running a full-scale hospital, and staff there actively promoted the cause of votes for women to patients and new staff alike.

Daisy Wadling died at Endell Street. Her coffin was covered with a Union flag and carried, with her military cap on top, to her funeral in Dorking by ASC bearers. After the funeral service, conducted by the vicar of St Paul's, a firing party of local volunteers fired in salute. It would have gratified the women of the Endell Street Hospital to see the local paper comment that 'We cannot but feel that the services so nobly rendered by the women of England for their country are worthy of all honour and gratitude.' The very fact that a military funeral could be held for a woman in a small market town indicates the changes in women's lives, and acceptance of their emancipation, that the war had brought.

Daisy's sister Ellen also played an active part in the war. She was a nurse at St Thomas's Hospital when war broke out. She volunteered for active service and crossed to France with the first British Expeditionary Force and remained there for the duration of the war. Ellen was Mentioned in Dispatches for gallant conduct and was awarded the RRC (Royal Red Cross) and the Mons Star.

'Sammy' Soane and Edith Withall

Samsbury Soane, seen here with two friends who are not in uniform, was originally from Farnborough, Hampshire. In France with the British Expeditionary Force, 'Sammy' was a machine-gunner with the Royal Berkshire Regiment. He sent pencil-written embroidered cards back home to Edith Withall, a nurse at Dorking Cottage Hospital. One reads 'from your loving sweet heart, Sammy, forget me not'; another 'from one who loves you, do not forget him'. The Christmas card depicts early military aircraft.

Sammy's family still has the rosary he was given while he was marching through a French village; the woman who gave it to him

said that it would keep him safe. He spent much of the war in a prisoner of war camp.

Edith was born in Leatherhead and was living in Dorking with her parents and brother when she received the cards from Sammy. They both survived the war but did not marry.

Three embroidered cards sent back to Edith Withall in Dorking, plus the reverse face of one card.

CHAPTER 7

Memorials and Remembrances

Returning soldiers found things changed. With shortages of manpower, draught animals and fuel, farmers had struggled. The grand houses had lost their staff, their gardens and greenhouses planted with necessities. Even after the end of hostilities, food remained scarce. Illness also continued: at Holmwood School there were so many children absent in November 1918 that the medical officer closed the school for two weeks. Sickness was endemic. Not only were people suffering from the influenza epidemic that killed more people worldwide than the war, but they were also required to notify the authorities of cases of diphtheria.

Those who served did not return home immediately. Demobilization was some time coming and prisoners of war took months to reach home. Leonard Roberts, who had been a prisoner of war, did not arrive home to take up his jobs with St Paul's and the Dorking British schools until January 1919; John Steeds, the headmaster of Newdigate School, only returned in February; and teacher Mr W.L. Crawley did not arrive back at his post at the British School until the March

W. Rich and K. Browell in fake beards for the fancy dress celebrations for the Armistice in 1919.

A wagon decorated for the peace celebrations of 17 July 1919.

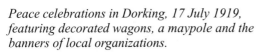

Reg and Ethel Betteridge dressed up to celebrate the Armistice in 1919. Fancy dress, cross-dressing and blacking-up were common features of celebrations and parades.

Peace celebrations in Dorking, 17 July 1919, featuring decorated wagons, a maypole and the banners of local organizations.

A decorated wagon
flying the English and
Union flags at the town
peace celebrations, 17
July 1919.

Peace celebration
procession on Dorking
High Street, looking
towards Pump Corner,
17 July 1919.

This procession is thought to be either for the peace celebrations in July 1919 or an Armistice Day in 1919 or 1920.

The Ancient Order of Foresters' peace celebrations at the Oddfellows Hall on Dorking High Street, 1919.

following the Armistice, having served in France, Salonika, Egypt and Palestine.

As the troops returned home there were celebrations and parties, but peace was not formally celebrated until 17 July 1919 when the town put aside a weekend for celebrations. There was a procession of bands and decorated wagons through streets hung with bunting and flags, a thanksgiving service, sports competitions, a children's tea and a choral concert. On 1 October the village of Capel held a 'Welcome Home' dinner programme for the 'Capel Contingent'. Around 100 with connections to the village who had served sat down to a feast of roast beef and pork, salads, apple and blackberry tarts, jellies and blancmange, cheese and beer. Each man was presented with a silver token of the village's gratitude. On 11 November 1919, the first anniversary of the Armistice, the first Remembrance Day was observed. It was recorded that at St Paul's School children massed at 10.45am. The king's address was read, followed by a brief address on the meaning of observance; then began the first two-minute silence.

1914–1918.

RETURN

of the

CAPEL CONTINGENT.

"Welcome Home."

Menu for the 'Welcome Home' dinner prepared by the village of Capel for the return of the 'Capel Contingent' in October 1919.

Some 700,000 British men had lost their lives. The sons of master and servant had served and died. Sydney Hack of The Knoll lost his son, Adrian. The Habershons of Brook Lodge lost Philip and Sidney; Hugo Molesworth Legge of Holmwood Lodge was killed, while the Heaths of Anstie Grange lost Raymond Leopold Grieg Heath and Martin Heath Caldwell (grandson of Sir Leopold and of Colonel Helsham Jones). Canon Chichester, vicar of St Martin's, lost his son, as did Reverend Bird of Newdigate. Lieutenant Commander Thomas Edmund Harrison, son of Commander Matthew James Harrison and of Lucy Wedgwood of Leith Hill Place and his brother Lieutenant Commander George Basil Harrison were both killed. Henry Lee-Steere of Jayes Park lost his only

A silver badge was awarded to each of the serving men of Capel at a celebratory dinner in October 1919.

child. Mrs Janson of Newdigate Place lost two sons, and Lord Ashcombe of Denbies lost his three eldest boys. At Dorking British School the headmaster lost his only son (Captain A.N. Cousin, who had been training as an engineer in Sheffield when war broke out); the son of the school's benefactor, T. Edmund Powell, was also killed. In all, 10 to 15 per cent of those who served lost their lives.

It is perhaps ironic that those most involved in recruiting and encouraging others to enlist – the landowners, the head teachers and the local clergy – were more likely to lose their own sons, for the casualty rate among officers (as the educated sons of the pillars of the community became) was higher than that of the general ranks. It is this that gives rise to the 'Lost Generation' myth, for proportionally more of the educated and well-connected were killed and it was from that class that the leaders of the future would have been drawn. That the wealthy had the funds to commemorate their losses in public – on plaques and in stained-glass windows – contributes to the impression of a whole generation being wiped out.

It is hardly possible to say exactly how many of those who died came from or had strong connections to the Dorking area. Record-keeping was ad hoc, in the hands of parish magazines, friendly societies and school headmasters, with overlaps and omissions. The installation of war memorials was not a scientific, well-researched business, and differing criteria applied for inclusion from village to village. In some the fallen had to have been born in, or lived in, the village; in others the link could be tenuous, for example having a mother who had moved to the village or coming from a family that owned land in the area. Some of the fallen are commemorated in multiple memorials: in churches, schools and voluntary organizations. Others – and particularly those who died after 1920 but of wounds sustained during the war – are not commemorated at all. Some who appear on memorials were not dead after all but marrying and fathering children years after inclusion on those memorials.

There are 269 names listed on the Dorking town war memorial on South Street. A memorial was first proposed in July 1918, even before the war ended. There was debate as to whether it ought to be on consecrated or unconsecrated ground, but eventually a town centre site was selected. In July 1919 a call went out for subscriptions for funds. It was proposed that a 'roll of honour' should not just commemorate

the dead but should record all women who had done war work, as well as members of medical, legal and clerical professions who had worked in the war effort. However, in the end it was only the male dead who were recorded.

The Dorking War Memorial unveiling and dedication took place on Sunday, 17 July 1921, the anniversary of the first peace celebrations. A crowd of 3,000 attended. It was an extremely hot day and the *Dorking and Leatherhead Advertiser* noted that 'the intense heat was extremely disconcerting'. Many were overcome. The town band played *Land of Hope and Glory* before the service began at 3pm with the local choral society and choirs singing the national anthem. Mr Beetham-Wilson addressed the crowd. Then followed a two-minute silence. A reading by Reverend Loton Parry, vicar of St Paul's, was followed by prayers led by Canon Chichester of St Martin's, whose son's name appeared on the memorial. The dedication by Lord Ashcombe was even more poignant as he had lost three sons. After prayers led by Reverend Grantham, *The Last Post* and *Reveille* were sounded. Wreaths were laid by the committee, the council and relatives of the dead. The ceremony concluded with the *Hallelujah Chorus* and a peal of bells from St Martin's. Immediately afterwards a hailstorm moved in, bringing the first rain for more than two months.

It had been proposed that Holmwood men be included on the Dorking war memorial; the names of North Holmwood men are to be found there. However, South Holmwood decided to form a committee of its own in order to raise money for a separate memorial. Designed by Sir Montague Omanay of Redlands and standing at the roadside to the east of the dual carriageway, the memorial to the twenty-seven men of South Holmwood who died was dedicated shortly after Dorking's, on 9 October 1921. Late in the day an approach was made to the committee to include the name of Victor Tickner, the gardener of Brook House who

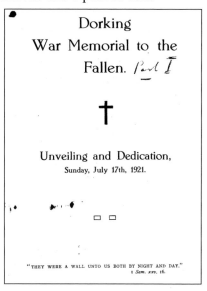

Dorking
War Memorial to the
Fallen. *Part I*

†

Unveiling and Dedication,
Sunday, July 17th, 1921.

□ □

"THEY WERE A WALL UNTO US BOTH BY NIGHT AND DAY."
1 *Sam. xxv, 16.*

Programme for the unveiling of the Dorking War Memorial in South Street, 17 July 1921.

The ceremonial dedication and unveiling of the Dorking War Memorial, 17 July 1921. The shorter of the two men in full morning dress is J. Beetham Wilson, Dorking chemist and chair of the War Memorial Committee; the other is Thomas Grantham, the minister of Dorking Congregational Church. The naval officer is Lord Anson and the man in military dress is Lord Ashcombe of Denbies. The Church of England ministers are the Reverend Loton Parry of St Paul's Church and Canon Chichester of St Martin's.

Crowds gathered to witness the unveiling of the Dorking War Memorial on 17 July 1921. The bandstand can be seen behind the memorial, looking north-east towards Pump Corner and Ranmore.

The bandstand stood in South Street, to the north of the War Memorial. It was dedicated by Charles Edmund Hall to his fellow townsmen who suffered and died in 1914–18 and in gratitude for victory. The bandstand has since been demolished. The plaque that commemorated the dedication of Dorking bandstand can now be seen in Dorking Museum.

TO THE MEMORY OF HIS FELLOW-TOWNSMEN WHO SUFFERED AND DIED FOR THEIR COUNTRY (1914-1918). AND IN GRATITUDE FOR VICTORY. THIS BAND-STAND IS DEDICATED BY CHARLES EDMUND HALL

had died of septic pneumonia in April 1916, two weeks after having cut his throat in a fit of insanity. It was unanimously agreed to include his name. Further south the village of Capel discussed commemorating the dead in more practical ways – by founding a village social centre or boys' club, erecting a clock tower, buying a recreation ground or bringing electric light to the village – before unveiling a memorial to the thirty-three who had lost their lives in 1921.

Schools, village halls and meeting places elected to commemorate

their dead. In South Holmwood a tablet incorporating three additional names to those on the village war memorial was placed in the church of St Mary Magdalene; a framed copy was presented to the next of kin by local Boy Scouts. Rolls of honour were placed in the village hall and, in September 1922, the school unveiled its own memorial. A further seventeen lives are commemorated in North Holmwood church. Schools generally put up their own memorials to lost former pupils. The Dorking British School managers 'would have failed in their duty had they omitted to place in the school a permanent record of the splendid devotion and heroic sacrifice of the lads who unhesitatingly gave themselves at their country's call,' wrote the headmaster Mr Cousin in 1920, in language reminiscent of 1914. It was a matter of pride with the school, and at no point is there any sense of disquiet that the boys' education should have been for this. Such doubts were seldom expressed in the immediate post-war years of relief and national celebration where small children still drilled and formed military bands and communities came together to honour their dead. At the British School Miss Corderoy arranged the provision of an illuminated inscription: a former pupil made a walnut frame, the headmaster carved the frame and Dorking artist Charles Collins (who, like the headmaster, had lost a son) assisted in preparation of the canvas. Like other local memorials, the British School's memorial to the thirty-one who did not return was paid for by subscription. It was unveiled by Miss Corderoy on the school's birthday in October 1920. It would serve, wrote Mr Cousin, 'to succeeding generations of scholars, a strong appeal to courage and devotion, and cannot fail to move all who see it to duty and self-sacrifice in the cause of humanity.' So was this most terrible of wars incorporated into the everyday life of the school and of the community.

The spirit of 1914 may have lingered in the language of memorials but life in the town and villages had changed, socially, economically and physically. Some of the divides in society in 1914 had been resolved. Women's suffrage, so divisive an issue in the local paper and at meetings in the years before the war, ceased to be such a point of disagreement. In 1918 women over the age of 30 who met certain property requirements were granted the vote in a reform act aimed primarily at granting the vote to servicemen, many of whom had not been eligible to vote before the war. This was not as contentious as it

The Dorking British School roll of honour was published in the school's annual reports for 1918. The juxtaposition of the list of old boys of the school who had been killed in 1914–18 with their contemporary May Queens is a poignant reminder of the differing expectations of males and females and their fates both in and on leaving school. It is also a reminder that as the young men fought and died, life went on at school much as it had before the war. It was this civilian incomprehension of the reality of war among civilians at home that writers such as Siegfried Sassoon and Robert Graves found so hard to cope with when they came home on leave. Dorking High School's casualty list was much longer, being a larger secondary school.

The Dorking British School roll of honour was unveiled in October 1920, on the anniversary of the school's foundation.

IN MEMORIAM.

Army.

Captain A. N. Cousin	Private P. Meadows
2nd-Lieut. W. Jeal	„ B. New
„ H. G. Stokes	„ W. Oliver
Sergeant H. Wright	„ R. Peters
Corporal Edgar Buckee	„ W. Razell.
„ P. W. Heal	„ D. Robinson
Gunner Wm. Lockyer	„ T. Stemp
Private R. Edmondson	„ A. Skett
„ D. Ford	„ W. H. Tickner
„ H. Gilbert	„ S. Townsend
„ F. Heal	„ C. Upfold
„ N. Jeater	„ S. Watts
„ A. Martin	„ Job Tickner
	„ W. Stanbridge.

Navy.

R. Boggis	F. Gale
A. Gale	R. Pledge

" His servants shall serve Him and they shall see His face."

MILITARY HONOURS (received in 1918).
M.C.—2nd-Lieut. J. B. Stokes.
M.M.—Rifleman T. H. Beesley.

MAY QUEENS.

1896	Nellie Walker	1908	Maggie Jeal
1897	Gertrude Field	1909	Dorothy Plummer
1898	Maggie Seabrook	1910	Nora Marshall
1899	Edith Marshall	1911	Madge Williams
1900	Lucy Marshall	1912	Daisy Watson
1901	Alice Geall	1913	Nellie George
1902	Maggie Tanner	1914	Gladys Rapley
1903	Gertrude Scragg	1915	Mabel Copp
1904	Elsie Warner	1916	Mercy Hollands
1905	Florence Lake	1917	Irene Thorogood
1906	Elsie Simmonds	1918	Phyllis Jacobs
1907	Emily Lake		

Mr Cousin, headmaster of Dorking British School, prepared the canvas for the school memorial. He had lost a son to the war.

The memorial in the village of Westcott.

The parents of Hugo Molesworth Legge set his memorial 'Dead Man's Penny' into a pew at St John's Church, North Holmwood. Hugo was the son of Lieutenant Colonel Edward Legge of the Coldstream Guards, assistant Sergeant-at-Arms at the House of Commons, and his wife Cordelia Molesworth Twysden Legge. He grew up at Holmwood Lodge, opposite the church. He was killed in 1915, aged 24. His brother Montague Bentinck Legge DSO (later Admiral) captained HMS Nerissa at the Battle of Jutland in 1916.

Women like Edith Sheppard had seen their lives and opportunities transformed by the war as they took up previously 'male' occupations. Edith had been one of the first women stationmasters at Ardingly in West Sussex before she became Mrs Cyril Turner in Dorking. Her father had been the stationmaster at Ockley. At the end of the war many returned to traditional roles, but they had changed others' attitudes towards women's capabilities.

once might have been: in the war years the people of Dorking had seen women at work on the land, running businesses and voluntary organizations, doing postal rounds, installing telephones, being decorated for their services overseas, and a full military funeral had been given to the daughter of an army officer in the heart of the community. However, with the coming of peace some traditional roles reasserted themselves. For example, in the Dorking British School yearbook for 1918 the dead for the years 1914–18 were listed alongside the May Queens for the corresponding years.

Despite this progression, other rifts in the community had opened as travel and contact with new ideas changed attitudes, particularly with regard to relations between the mass of ordinary people and their social betters. During the debates about registration and conscription, letters to the paper had criticized the patrician disposal by the well-to-do of the lives of their employees, the National Union of Railwaymen had been vocal in promoting the interests of working people on the Military Tribunal, and a trade union for agricultural labourers had been established in Newdigate. Peace returned men to town and villages less willing to bow to the wishes of their elders and social betters. Often returning soldiers formed close bonds with others who had served and who understood their experiences. In South Holmwood there was something of a crisis at the village club in 1920 when the ex-soldiers football team of the Comrades of the Great War asked that alcohol be

Nellie Peters from Dorking in the uniform of the Chilworth Gunpowder Works, 1916. Her 'On War Work' triangular badge can be clearly seen. Born in 1891, by the age of 9 Nellie was an inmate at Dorking Workhouse with her five brothers and sisters. By 1911 she was working as a servant at the Black Horse public house on the High Street in Dorking. During the war Nellie took up war work at the gunpowder works that had been established at Chilworth in the seventeenth century. It was a dangerous occupation, and not just on account of the explosives that women like Nellie were handling. The nearby church was camouflaged to prevent enemy Zeppelins using it to navigate towards the factory and in 1915 a series of bombs was dropped on Guildford as a Zeppelin pilot attempted to identify the works.

served. This would have been unthinkable before the war as the club had been built on land donated by the late Reverend Wickham, but even in 1920 the Reverend's son, who was living in Somerset, had more say in the running of the club than the villagers who used it. He agreed that a 'wet canteen' would be acceptable if it was not run for profit. However, others in the community felt they had a duty to protect the morality of the 'lower orders', notwithstanding their service in the war. Anne Garrett of Holm Cottage referred the matter to her solicitor, claiming that 'many who would shrink from going to a public house will have no scruples in drinking at the Hall, the fact that the authorities permit drink there will make it appear quite natural and right'. It would be leading the young of both sexes into temptation, she claimed.

Perhaps change was most obviously to be seen in the great mansions that surrounded the town. Many had seen military or hospital use; most had been neglected, their owners suddenly faced with running and maintenance with reduced funds and without an army of low-paid

Comrades of the Great War membership certificate. The Comrades of the Great War was formed in 1917 to represent the interests of ex-servicemen and women. It was one of the organizations that amalgamated to form the British Legion in 1921. In the face of hardship on their return from the war, ex-servicemen banded together, establishing local branches to provide comradeship and support.

DEEPDENE, DORKING. 75292 (N)

Deepdene never returned to residential use after the war but became a hotel in the 1920s.

servants. Though most did revert to family use, the day of the great house was in decline as many who had experienced other work during the war never went back to the restrictions of domestic service. Many of the large estates surrounding Dorking were auctioned in lots in the post-war years, being more valuable as potential building land for housing. Deepdene, once an employer of hundreds in its farms, gardens, stables and mansion, never returned to residential use. In the 1920s its lands were sold off and it became a hotel, catering to the thousands who would come down to the Surrey Hills with the advent of mass tourism in the 1920s.

War-related hardship continued well after the war. The Dorking War Emergency Relief Sub-Committee was replaced by the Dorking War Emergency Fund in 1921 and it was still making payments to those whose financial hardship was attributable to the war into the 1930s to enable widows and the war-wounded to buy groceries and coal. Far from finding jobs open to them over those who had not voluntarily enlisted as promised in 1914, those returning wounded often found they could get no work at all; conscription and the passage of time had blurred memories of who had gone to war voluntarily.

In addition to living expenses, those who had been wounded found themselves facing medical bills and the costs of transport to take

themselves to related appointments. Such costs could not be met by men with little, lowly-paid, or no work at all and there was no state-funded care for those who had fought and been injured. The sick and the dying found themselves dependent on charity. The Dorking War Emergency Fund was called upon to pay for taxis to take the war disabled to London hospitals, to refund ambulance charges for ex-servicemen taken in to local hospitals, and to provide nurses to tend patients in their homes. The fund also dispensed an annual Christmas gift of a new half-crown to each of the town's war orphans, for which the scheme was responsible. The orphans' fund also took care of uniforms and apprenticeship fees for the children when they came to leave school.

There were many applications to the fund in the 1920s as war veterans sought to re-establish their civilian lives. An application to buy a horse and cart to allow one ex-serviceman to start a firewood business was declined as not being a proper use of funds; in general the fund attempted to find employment for those it was supporting, rather than supporting them to establish themselves in business. However, in 1924 it was still struggling to find training for work that could be undertaken by one-armed Mr Jordan who could not afford boots for his children and who, according to his doctors, needed 'expensive apparatus' for his leg and arm. Another ex-serviceman, Mr DeVoil, needed money to buy an artificial hand.

The fund's records reveal the slow toll of the war on those who had served, with sick men dying early into the 1920s, others in hospitals undergoing operations or in sanatoriums, and therefore unable to work. Some, like the one-armed Mr Jordan, claimed charity from multiple providers: the Poor Law Guardians, the Emergency Relief Fund and the Oddfellows (Mr Jordan eventually died in 1927, his circumstances not improved, and the fund had to make a grant of £5 to his daughter to meet funeral expenses). The incapacity of the family breadwinner often plunged whole families into poverty and the deaths of ex-servicemen saw families broken up: in 1923 Mr Edwards' daughter applied to the fund on her father's death for an outfit and rail ticket to live with her married sister in the Midlands (and for the expense of the nurse who tended her father when he died). Medical expenses for the treatment of war injuries were a constant drain on the families of those who survived long after the war. The question of ambulance fees

Poppy Day in Dorking High Street, 1921.

Whit Monday on Ranmore, 1919. Crowds watch the flag flying in the first spring of peacetime.

charged by the Red Cross for conveying ex-servicemen to London hospitals for treatment became so pressing that in 1925 the committee sought a meeting with the Red Cross, suggesting a waiver of fees for these men. In a country with no universal health-care system, the war raised questions in the minds of many as to the contract between the citizen who found himself called upon to fight in time of crisis but was little supported by the state in his resultant adversity. It would take another war for those issues to be fully examined and addressed.

In 1919 four members of the British delegation to the Peace Conference in Paris visited Leith Hill tower. By 1920 the tower, that had received just a dribble of visitors during the war, was receiving 500 visitors a week in summer, marking the advent of mass tourism. It must have seemed to those who climbed the tower that the war – and perhaps all war – was well behind them. However, the treaty agreed by those visiting delegates to conclude 'the war to end all wars' brought only a short peace. Within twenty years the tower would once again be providing respite from a European war to servicemen in uniform.

The Dorking High School Officer Training Corps Band, c.1921. At the end of the war the military continued to be held in high esteem and military traditions that had been prevalent in wartime continued into the 1920s.

Memorial service at Dorking War Memorial following the death of Douglas, 1st Earl Haig, commander of the British army for much of the war. In later decades Haig's reputation has been called into question. However, Haig was held in great esteem as the man who won the war when he died in 1928 and crowds turned out for the memorial service.

The Cubitt Boys

Henry Cubitt (1867–1947) inherited the title of 2nd Lord Ashcombe in 1917. He was the grandson of Thomas Cubitt, the master builder of Victorian London, and had served as Lord Lieutenant of Surrey. On the death of his father he moved his family to Denbies, the mansion that the great builder had had constructed for himself in the 1850s. Henry Cubitt's wife, Maud Marianne nee Calvert, had grown up at Ockley Court, a few miles to the south of the town. The couple had six sons.

Henry Archibald Cubitt (1892–1916) was the first of Lord Ashcombe's sons to be killed. The story is told that one of the Cubitt sons was riding near the front when he saw a stretcher party who had been ordered to carry away the body of an officer of a family said to be of some importance. On asking to see the body, he found it was his brother. (Portrait by Lance Calkin)

A committed imperialist, Lord Ashcombe had served as a volunteer in the Queen's (Royal West Surrey) Regiment with the local Dorking Company. He had later been responsible for raising the Surrey (The Princess of Wales) Imperial Yeomanry, providing a rifle range for them at Pickett's Hole on Ranmore. When war broke out he was a committed recruiter, speaking on the streets and at the weekly market. Several of his own sons were already serving with the regular army.

Henry Cubitt's eldest son, Captain Henry Archibald Cubitt (1892–1916) of the Coldstream Guards, was killed on 15 September 1916. On the death of his heir, Lord Ashcombe applied to convert the transept of St Barnabas' church on Ranmore into a chapel in his memory (the family had built the church for the Denbies estate). However, by the time permission had been granted in 1917, Henry's brothers – Lieutenant Alick George Cubitt (1894–1917) of the 15th Hussars and Lieutenant William Hugh Cubitt of the 1st Royal Dragoons – had also been killed. The chapel became a memorial to

the three brothers and the title of 3rd Lord Ashcombe was finally inherited (in 1947) by the fourth brother, Roland, who had never been expected to inherit.

The Cubitt Chapel at St Barnabas was consecrated by the Bishop of Winchester in June 1919. On the door is a simple wooden cross taken from the grave of the eldest brother. The altar and pavement in memory of Henry are in Greek marble; tablets on either side commemorate his brothers. Murals on the wall by E. Reginald Frampton (1872–1923) depict the Madonna with the Wise Men, Faith, Hope and Charity, Peace, Justice and Fortitude, and the patron saints of England, France and Belgium.

The Cubitt Chapel, St Barnabas Church, Ranmore. (Image reproduced by courtesy of a commons creative licence)

Eleven other parishioners were killed in the war and a plaque to their memory was dedicated in June 1922. The boys' cousin, Captain William George Cubitt Chichester of the 1st London Regiment, was also killed, in September 1916 at High Wood during the Delville Wood offensive on the Somme. His mother was Lord Ashcombe's sister, Mary Ann, and his father was the vicar of St Martin's in Dorking, Canon Edward Chichester.

A Peace Celebration Romance

William Dinnage (1900–82) missed the war. He left school in May 1914 as his parents could not afford for him to stay on, and began work as an agricultural labourer with his father. As a 16-year-old he claimed to have seen a 'fireball' moving across the sky while out working in the fields. A superstitious friend took it as an omen. Excited when he was called up in June 1918, he had not left England when the Armistice was declared in November. He spent the rest of the year with the Army of Occupation in Germany, and on returning home re-enlisted in February 1919 as there was a scarcity of work at home for returning soldiers.

Dinnage met his future wife at the victory celebrations in July 1919 at Deepdene while on leave before setting out with his regiment for India. He went on to produce many drawings of Dorking that are now in Dorking Museum's collection.

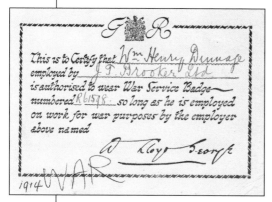

William Dinnage's Certificate of War Service. The badge that would have been issued with the certificate indicated that the wearer was on war service, so explaining why he had not enlisted. It was issued to Dinnage when he was working at Taylor and Brooke's timber yard near Dorking Station.

The timber yard on Station Road, Dorking where William Dinnage worked. Photographed before the war, it expanded during the war years when providing timber from the hills around the town was vital to the war effort.

Bibliography

Publications:

Anon, *Dorking Cemetery, Reigate Road, Dorking, Surrey: Guide to Notable Graves in Dorking's Historic Cemetery*

Anon, *Music Won the Cause: 100 Years of the Leith Hill Musical Festival 1905–2005* (2005)

Atherton, Kathy, *The Lost Villages: A History of the Holmwoods* (2008)

Atherton, Kathy, *The Museum Guide to Dorking* (2013)

Callcut, John, *A Village at War: Newdigate in World War One* (2011)

Chesney, Sir George, *The Battle of Dorking* (1871)

Dinnage, William, *Recollections of Old Dorking* (1977)

Ettlinger, Vivien, *The Holloway Dorking: Medieval Farm to Modern Estate* (1997)

Ettlinger, Vivien, Jackson, Alan A. & Overell, Brian, *Dorking: A Surrey Market Town Through Twenty Centuries* (1992)

Fortescue, S.E.D., *The House on the Hill: The Story of Ranmore and Denbies* (1993)

Holland, Coffey, *Dorking People* (1984)

Horne, Susannah, *Mr Finlay's Cottages: The Making of Myrtle Road* (2012)

Jackson, Alan, *Dorking's Railways* (1991)

Newbery, Celia, (ed.), *Vaughan Williams in Dorking* (1979)

Tarplee, Peter, *Railways Around Leatherhead and Dorking* (2011)

Wedgwood, Alexandra A., *History of St Martin's, Dorking* (1990)

Wharmby, Helen, *A History of St Paul's School* (2013)

Primary sources:

Letters, diaries, programmes, news cuttings, posters and other ephemera at Dorking Museum and Surrey History Centre

Capel Notes, the Journal of Capel Local History Group
Dorking British School Annual Reports
Dorking High School termly reports
Dorking History, the Journal of Dorking Local History Group
Dorking and Leatherhead Advertiser 1914–19
Holmwood Parish Magazines 1914
Kelly's Directory 1913–14
Minutes of the Dorking Military Tribunal 1916–18
Minutes of the Dorking Relief Sub-Committee of the Dorking
   Emergency Committee
Minutes of the Dorking War Emergency Fund
Minute books of the Dorking Urban District Council 1917–19
Minute books of the Holmwood War Memorial Committee
Surrey Advertiser 1914–19
The Holmesdale Directory 1913–14

Index

Abinger, 9, 33, 36, 46, 48, 53, 85, 94, 140
  Abinger Hall, 17, 84, 85, 103
Anti-German feeling, 47–8
  Degenhardt, Charles, 24, 47–8
  spying fears, 64, 79
Armistice and peace celebrations, 150,
  154–6, 163–7, 184

Battle of Dorking, the, 21, 29, 96
Beare Green, 9, 35, 53, 58, 83, 85, 88,
  94, 107, 115, 140
  Prosecuting Society, demise of, 83
Betchworth, 9, 15, 17, 26–7, 33, 85, 93,
  101, 136, 140
  Betchworth Park and Golf Club, 15,
  17, 26, 68
Box Hill, 9, 11, 14–15, 21, 24, 27, 30,
  40, 45, 52, 59, 74, 95, 100, 160
  Burford Bridge Hotel, 24, 43, 100
  Burford Lodge, 140, 142
Boy Scouts, 26, 32, 44, 53, 84, 158, 172
Brockham, 9, 33, 90, 140
  Broome Park 90, 136

Capel, 9, 17, 33, 35, 39, 51, 53, 56, 95–
  6, 109, 140, 148, 156, 167, 171
  Lyne House 17, 156
  Wattlehurst Farm, 109, 148
Chilworth Gunpowder Works, 175
Churches,
  Christ Church, Coldharbour, 65–6
  Congregational Church and Hall
  (Dorking), 56, 74, 170
  St Barnabas', Ranmore, 182–3
  St John's, North Holmwood, 58, 172,
  174

St Martin's, Dorking, 12, 33, 60, 74–
  5, 83, 113, 123, 126, 152, 157, 167,
  169, 183
St Mary Magdalene, South
  Holmwood, 31, 72
St Paul's, Dorking, 61, 161, 169–70
St Peter's, Newdigate, 54
Coldharbour, 9, 17, 22, 33, 35, 44, 49,
  63, 65–6, 93, 126–7, 140, 154
Comrades of the Great War, 175–6
Conscription and opposition to it, 22–3,
  41–2, 54, 65, 80, 86, 88–91, 106–109,
  111, 120, 146, 151, 175, 177
  registration, 89–91, 106, 108, 175
  Military Tribunal, 65, 91, 106–109,
  118, 147–8, 151, 175
  see also Pethick-Lawrence, Frederick

Dorking,
  clubs and civic organisations:
    effect of manpower shortages, 80,
    111, 118, 135, 152
    Dorking and District Rifle Club, 22,
    27, 53, 64
    Dorking and District Whippet
    Racing Association, 27
    Dorking Boy Scouts, 26, 32, 84,
    158, 172
    Dorking Chamber of Commerce,
    46–7
    Dorking Cricket Club, 17–18, 27,
    43, 111, 117
    Ladies Team, 113
    Dorking Fire Brigade and Fire
    Station, 17, 83
    Dorking Football Club, 17, 42–4, 157

Dorking Imperial Club, 17, 26
Dorking town band, 17, 26, 29, 33,
    35–6, 47, 52, 140, 154, 158, 169
National Union of Railway men,
    Dorking branch 17, 107, 138–9, 175
Old Paulonians' Cycle Club, the, 28
Surrey Union Hunt, 65
governance,
    Dorking and District Committee of
        the Women's Branch of the Board
        of Agriculture *see* women's roles
    Dorking Defence Committee and
        Surrey Defence Committee, 52–3,
        93–5, 111
    see also invasion fears and evacuation
        plans
    Dorking Rural District Council, 17
    Dorking Urban District Council, 17,
        33, 45, 46, 51, 56, 78, 80, 89, 116,
        158
mansions surrounding the town,
    decline after the war, 176–7
    Anstie Grange, 17, 24, 35, 49, 53,
        58, 63–6, 77, 107, 126–8, 154, 167
    see also Hospitals, Heath, Cuthbert
    Bury Hill, 15–16, 45, 59, 84, 135
    Deepdene, 15–16, 58
        Troops billeted, 58–9, 68–71, 101,
            110, 135, 177, 184
    Denbies, 15–16, 30, 33, 39, 58, 68,
        78, 85, 95–6, 120, 135, 168, 170,
        182
    Norbury Park, 15, 40
    Pippbrook, 140, 141
    Sondes Place, 58, 68, 78, 116, 131
public spaces and meeting places,
    Congregational Hall, 74
    Cotmandene, 25–6, 113
    Falkland Arms, 36, 137
    Glory Wood, 15
    Nower, the, 15, 45
    Oddfellows' Hall, 55, 57, 75, 166
    Public Halls, 19, 58, 68, 103, 140, 152
    Red Lion Hotel, 12, 37–8, 43, 154,
        158, 160

Queen's Head ,77
Station Hotel, 77
Surrey Yeoman Inn, 23
Wesleyan Hall, 57, 59, 71
White Horse Hotel, 58, 155
schools,
    British School, 18, 42, 46, 49–50,
        60, 83, 110, 112, 131–4, 139–40,
        142, 163, 168, 172–3, 175
    High School, 25, 50, 91–2, 117,
        134, 152–3, 173, 181
    St Martin's School, 89, 157
    St Paul's School, 28, 42, 60, 111,
        118, 123, 125, 139, 152, 163, 167
town in 1914, 9–25
troops billeted in the town, 67–79,
    80–2
    Argyll and Sutherland Highlanders,
        78, 89
    Civil Service Rifles, 64, 68, 71, 77,
        109, 144
    London Scottish (London
        Regiment), 68, 70–5, 77, 79, 80
    Royal Army Medical Corps
        (London Regiment), 68, 74–6, 103
    Royal Army Service Corps, 77, 81,
        160
    Royal Field Artillery (London
        Regiment), 50, 68, 78, 125
    Surrey Yeomanry, 16, 24, 52, 55,
        58–9, 67–70, 78, 80, 140, 142
war-related initiatives,
    adoption of HMS *Titania*, 155
    anti-aircraft hooter, 91–2
    Hospital Supply Depot, 84, 130, 139
    Voluntary Aid Detachments, 24, 58
    Volunteer Training Corps, 53–4, 95
    War Emergency Relief Sub-
        committee and War Emergency
        Fund, 46, 136–7, 177–80
    Waste Paper Depot, 84, 130
wartime events,
    bank holiday athletic sports, 27–9
    Bronco Bill's Wild West Exhibition,
        25–6

Red Cross Week 1917, 139–43
War Weapons Week, 153

Food and fuel shortages and production
see also women's roles
  Belladonna growing, 131, 157
  fruit and conker gathering, 132, 152
  Kingham's store offers cheaper prices
    to families of those serving, 45
  price rises, 27, 45, 61, 84, 116, 119,
    132, 135, 137
  shortages and rationing, 119–20, 129–
    32, 150
Holmbury St Mary, 9, 120, 140
  prisoner of war camp, 122
Holmwood, 9, 11, 17, 31, 33, 35, 37–9,
  42, 44, 46–7, 49, 53, 55–6, 58, 60–1,
  63, 77, 83, 85, 88–9, 93–4, 98, 100,
  102, 104, 109, 111, 114–15, 119–20,
  123, 126, 136, 139–40, 144–7, 149,
  153, 167, 169, 172, 174–5
  Ancient Order of Foresters, 114, 118
  Holmwood Defence Committee,
    93–4, 111
  Norfolk Arms, 109, 114
  North Holmwood School, 99
  South Holmwood School, 42, 60, 109,
    112, 132, 134, 162–3
  Sundial, the, 56, 145, 149
  Village Club, 175
  Volunteer Fire Brigade, 83, 118–20
  wartime weddings, 88, 115
Hospitals,
  Anstie Grange Military Hospital, 66,
    126–8, 154
  Dorking Isolation Hospital, 121
  Dorking workhouse hospital, 97
  Kirkstall (Dorking), 58, 60

Illness and epidemics, 134, 163
Invasion fears and evacuation plans, 52–
  3, 91–6

Leigh, 39, 74, 89, 140
Leith Hill, 11, 14–15, 21, 56, 74, 112, 180

Leith Hill Musical Competitions, 83,
  85, 103
Leith Hill Place, 17, 68, 103, 114, 167
Licensing restrictions, 77, 95

Mickleham, 9, 27, 40, 44, 51, 53, 61, 84,
  95, 140
  Mickleham Hall, 54, 56, 95
  Mickleham School, 50, 111
  Volunteer fire brigade, 44, 84
Military Tribunal see Conscription and
  opposition to it

Newdigate, 9, 17, 27, 33, 36, 38, 46, 51,
  53–4, 60–2, 83, 85, 89, 95, 107, 110,
  116, 119, 122, 125, 130–1, 138, 140,
  150, 167, 175
  Cudworth smallholdings and holiday
    camp, 17, 27, 60, 91, 107, 109,
    147–8, 151
  Useful Service Brigade and Volunteer
    Company, 53–4, 95
  Newdigate Place, 53, 108, 143, 168
  Newdigate School, 42, 125, 134, 152,
    154, 162–3

Ockley, 9, 22, 33, 35, 53, 85, 96, 110, 174
Opposition to the War,
  Quakers, 37
  see also Pethick-Lawrence, Emmeline
    and Pethick-Lawrence, Frederick

Pixham, 9, 18, 27, 57

Queen's (Royal West Surrey) Regiment,
  the – see recruitment and enlisting

Ranmore, 9, 14–15, 21, 30, 33, 59, 74,
  78, 85, 94–5, 152, 170, 180, 182–3
Rationing – see food and fuel shortages
Recruitment and enlisting
  recruitment and rallies, 34–43, 47, 49,
    53–5, 64, 86, 89, 90, 96
  Queen's (Royal West Surrey) Regiment,
    31–2, 47, 49, 66, 89, 123, 182

Refugees,
    Belgian refugees, 56–7, 60–1, 145
    Zeppelin raid refugees, 137–9
Registration – see Conscription and
    opposition to it
Remembrance Day, 167, 179
Reservists, 23, 29, 31–2, 34, 45, 47, 50–
    1, 80, 111
    see also Surrey Yeomanry
Schools, see Dorking and individual
    villages
Special Constables, 52–3, 65, 83, 93–4,
    111, 118–19, 151

Territorials, 22–3, 25, 29, 31–3, 37, 42,
    45, 50–1, 58, 67, 68, 80, 111
    see also Queens (Royal West Surrey)
        Regiment
    Drill Hall, 10, 22, 30, 33, 37, 47,
        192

War memorials, 168–73
    Capel War Memorial, 171
    Cubitt Memorial Chapel, Ranmore,
        182–3
    Dorking bandstand, 170–1

Dorking British School War Memorial,
    172–3
Dorking South Street War Memorial,
    123, 131, 168–71, 181
North Holmwood War Memorials,
    169, 172, 174
South Holmwood War Memorials,
    123, 169, 171–2
St Martin's War Memorial, 123
Westcott War Memorial, 174
War Savings, 86, 134
Westcott, 9, 17, 27, 33, 46, 53, 78, 85,
    87, 140
    Milton Court, 131
    Milton Heath, 78
    rifle range and railway halt, 78
Westhumble, 9
Women's changing roles, 83, 112–16,
    152–3, 172, 175
    pre–war women's suffrage
        campaigns, 17, 55
    see also Emmeline-Pethick-Lawrence
    War Agricultural Service for Women,
        116, 152
Wotton, 9, 27, 33, 53, 140
    Wotton House, 19

Index of individuals and businesses named in the text

Ackland, George Henry, 38
Adams and Co., 45, 136
Aitcheson, John, 109, 148, 192
Anson, Lord, 170
Ashbourne, Lord, 56
Ashcombe, Lord, see Cubitt, Henry
Aston, Constance, 116
Attlee, E.W., 154

Baden Powell, Lord Robert, 14–15
Beetham-Wilson, J., 131, 154, 157,
    169–70
Betteridge, Reg and Ethel, 164

Bird, Rev, 54, 62, 74, 89, 95, 130, 150,
    167
Bixby, Bessie, 42
Blakeney, Dr Hugh, 36–7, 49, 113
Bowring, Stephen, 109
Bray, Gerard Theodore and Evelyn nee
    Broadwood, 38
Broadwood family, 17, 38
    Broadwood, Bertha, 17, 156
Browell, K., 163
Brooker's Timber Yard, 184
Bryans, Arthur and Annie, 153

Calvert, Felix, 96, 121
Chesney, Sir George , 29
Chester, Thomas Trueman, 123
Chichester, Canon Edward, 33, 60, 113,
    126, 167, 169–70, 183
Clark and Co., 61
Collins, Charles, 172
Corderoy, Miss, 172
Cousin, AN, 168
Cousin, Stephen, 112, 172–3
Crawley, W.L., 163
Cubitt family,
    Alick George Cubitt, 110, 182
    George Cubitt, 1st Lord Ashcombe,
        15–16, 22, 30, 33, 39
    Henry Cubitt. 2nd Lord Ashcombe,
        15–16, 33, 38–40, 49, 58–9, 89, 96,
        110, 120, 169–70, 182
    Henry Archibald Cubitt, 182–3
    Maud Marianne Cubitt, nee Calvert,
        96, 182
    Roland Cubitt, 182
    Thomas Cubitt, 15, 182
    William Hugh Cubitt, 182
Curry, Arthur Frederick, 47
Curtis, Bernard, 52

Dean, Alfred, 107–108
Degenhardt, Charles, 24, 47–8
Dinnage, William, 53–4, 120, 184
Donovan, P., 98
Dudley, Walter, 151

Farrer, Lord, 17, 24
Farrer, Evangeline, Lady, 24, 84–5, 103
Fielding, Sir Percy, Lady Louisa and
    Lisma, 136
Finley, Rev. William Russell, 26–7, 58

Gardiner, George, 46
Garrett, Anne, 176
Gibbs, Albert, 35
Gilbert, M., 98–9
Golding, William, 59
Gordon-Clark, H.H., 54

Gore-Brown, Doreen, 126
Grantham, Rev Thomas, 169–70
Green, Frederick Ernest, 53, 91, 119,
    139, 147–8

Habershon Family, 60, 167
Hack Family, 167
Haig, Sir Douglas, 63–4, 181
Hall, Charles Edmund, 171
Hampton, Lady Laura, 120
Hardy, Frank, 87
Harman Young,
    Henry, 62–3
    Kenneth, 109, 144
Harris, Ken, 87
Harris, Mr and Mrs Percy, 130
Harrison Family, 167
Heath family, 63–6, 126
    Arthur Raymond Heath, 65–6, 128
    Cuthbert Eden Heath, 17, 24, 35, 37,
        49, 53, 63–6, 77, 107, 126, 128
    Frederick Dunbar Heath, 128
    Genesta Heath, 49, 64–5, 126–7
    Gerard Moore Heath, Major General
        Sir, 63–4
    Herbert Heath, Admiral Sir, 63–4
    Leopold Heath, Admiral Sir Leopold,
        63, 167
    Martin Heath Caldwell, 167
    Raymond Leopold Grieg Heath, 65–6,
        167
Helsham-Jones, Henry H, 55, 88, 107,
    167
Hodges, W.L., 31
Hudson, Aubrey, 123–6

James, William, 77
Janson, Ellen, 53–4, 108, 168
Johns, Westley, 122
Jordan, Mr, 178

Kay, Doris, 119
Keep, Alfred, 147

Langdon-Davies, John, 149

Lawrence, Lady, 140, 142–3
Lee-Steere,
    Henry, 22, 35, 167
    John, 35
Legge Family
    Hugo Molesworth Legge, 167, 174
    Montague Bentinck Legge, 174
Livermore, Dora, 143, 156
Longman, Margaret, 84

Mackrell family, seven brothers serving, 42
Matthews, Len, 52
Mercer, James, 47
Morris, Frances, 42

Norfolk, Duke of, 56, 135

Omanay, Sir Montague, 169

Palmes, Canon, 31
Pardon-Howe, Mr, 34, 89
Parry, Rev Loton, 169–70
Peters, Nellie, 175
Pethick-Lawrence, Emmeline, 37, 55–6, 144–7
Pethick-Lawrence, Frederick, 109, 139, 144–5, 147–9
Phillips, Eric, 86, 116
Piper, Alan, 104
Powell, T. Edmund, 168
Pratt, Frank, 77
Priest, Mary, 90

Reader, Albert, 51
Rich, W., 163
R.J. Cook, 61
Roberts, Leonard, 163

Robertson, Charles VC, 157–60
Rose, G.K., 50
Rose, Mrs W.J., 84
Ryder, Lady Margaret, 27

Salomons, Leopold, 15, 40, 49
Sellick, Ernest, 108, 151
Shearburn, William, 87
Sheppard, Edith, 174
Simpson, Kate, 42
Skett, Alan, 47
Soane, 'Sammie' Samsbury, 161–2
Spencer Family, 88, 115
Strachey, Loe, 22, 41, 95
Stavridi, John, 104–105
Steeds, John, 42, 163
Stewart, Ann, 114
Strudwick, Lucy, 112
Strudwick, Valentine 'Joe', 123–5

Taylor, Edward, 51
Taylor, Kenneth, 117
Tickner, Victor, 123, 169, 171
Turner, Albert, 107
Turner, E.W., 109
Turner, Mrs and Miss, 115

Vanderbilt, Alfred Gwynne, 24, 99–102
Vaughan-Williams, Margaret, 103
Vaughan-Williams, Ralph, 68, 75, 103–104, 114
Vialls, Edmund, 91–2

Wadling, Daisy and Ellen, 160–1
Warne's Automobile repairers, 76–7
Withall, Edith, 161–2
Wylde, Alice, 134
Worrow, Maggie, 114